Library of
AFRICAN-AMERICAN HISTORY

Frontier of Freedom

AFRICAN AMERICANS IN THE WEST

LISA YOUNT

☑® Facts On File, Inc.

In memory of
GEORGE YOUNT,
also a western pioneer

Frontier of Freedom: African Americans in the West

Copyright © 1997 by Lisa Yount

Facts On File, Inc.
11 Penn Plaza
New York NY 10001

Library of Congress Cataloging-in-Publication Data

Yount, Lisa.
    Frontier of freedom : African Americans in the West / Lisa Yount.
        p.   cm. — (Library of African-American history)
    Includes bibliographical references and index.
    ISBN 0-8160-3372-2
        1. Afro-Americans—West (U.S.)—History. 2. Afro-Americans—West (U.S.)—Biography. 3. Frontier and pioneer life—West (U.S.)
    4. West (U.S.)—Race relations. I. Title. II. Series.
    E185.925.Y68 1997
    978'.00496073—dc21 96-46863

Facts On File books are available at special discounts when purchased in bulk quantities for businesses, associations, institutions or sales promotions. Please call our Special Sales Department in New York at 212/967-8800 or 800/322-8755.

Text design by Cathy Rincon
Cover design by Nora Wertz
Illustrations on pages 6, 72, 90, 129 by Facts On File Electronic Graphics

This book is printed on acid-free paper.
Printed in the United States of America

MP FOF 10 9 8 7 6 5 4 3 2 1

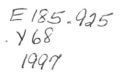
Contents

1

The West: Frontier of Freedom?

Most Americans know their story, not only from school textbooks but from countless books, movies, and TV shows about the American West:

Explorers, sighting what was to them a new land, ripe for both plunder and settlement.

Pioneers, struggling across the wilderness in wagon trains and braving angry Indians, parched deserts, and seemingly impassable mountain ranges.

Gold-rush miners, panning for riches in the sunny California countryside.

Soldiers, galloping over the rise just in time to save beleaguered families from attack.

Cowboys, driving herds of steers across the dusty plains and celebrating the end of the trail in wild cow towns.

Homesteaders, battling dust, wind, and grasshoppers and huddling in sod shanties, hoping that their hard work would eventually turn the wilderness into prosperous farms.

Town and city dwellers, bringing law, education, and civilization to a once untamed land.

These legendary figures star in the tale of the settling of the American West—or rather resettling, since American Indians had lived in western North America for centuries before European invaders appeared. This often-told story provides more than entertainment. Early in the twentieth century, Woodrow Wilson, a historian and political scholar who later became president of the United States, called the story of the advancing westward frontier "the central and determining fact of our national history. . . . The West is the great word of our history. The Westerner has been the type and master of our American life."

What most people *don't* know is that some of the players in this "central and determining" drama of westward settlement—some members of all the groups just mentioned —were black. African Americans, except perhaps for a few slaves or servants, are almost unheard of in traditional Western movies or novels. In the real West, however, they were there. Their numbers were small, in terms of both the total African-American population of their day and the total Western population. But, says historian Kenneth Wiggins Porter, "what is surprising and significant . . . is that they were as important on the frontier as they were—in some cases definitely out of proportion to their relative numbers."

Until recently, even most professional historians were unaware of

> W*hat is surprising and significant . . . is that [African Americans] were as important on the frontier as they were.*
>
> ◆
>
> —Kenneth Wiggins Porter

African-American contributions to western settlement. Pu-
litzer Prize–winning historian James Truslow Adams wrote
in 1943:

> The . . . Negroes who were brought here [to the United
> States] had among them many excellent qualities . . .
> even temper, affection, great loyalty . . . imitativeness,
> willingness to follow a leader or master . . . but . . .
> [these] were . . . not the qualities which . . . made
> good . . . frontiersmen. . . . Not only were the Negroes
> as unfitted by nature from becoming founders of com-
> munities on the frontier as, let us say the Scotch–Irish
> were pre-eminently fitted for it, but they had no chance
> [to found such communities].

Adams was wrong. African Americans did have the
chance, and they took that opportunity and made the most
of it. Some mapped lands that no one except American
Indians had ever seen before. Some walked clear across the
country to find new homes. Some made daring escapes from
bondage, often with the help of other African Americans.
Some fought the most experienced Indian warriors to a
standstill, and others joined and even became leaders in
Indian groups. Some African Americans made fortunes in the
West. Some founded towns or became highly respected figures in growing western cities.

European Americans slowly spread across North America
from east to west during the 19th century, fulfilling what they
saw as their "manifest destiny"—their obvious, God-given
right, even duty—to occupy and control the continent "from
sea to shining sea." During that time, the meaning of *West*
and *frontier* constantly changed. To the fledgling United
States at the beginning of the 19th century, bounded on the
west by the Mississippi River, the western frontier was the
unsettled Northwest Territory (later the states of Wisconsin,
Illinois, Michigan, Indiana, and Ohio) and the mountainous

Clara Brown is typical of the black pioneers who helped to settle the West. A former slave, she came to Colorado during the 1859 gold rush. She saved the money she earned by doing laundry and used it to reunite her family, scattered by slavery, and help other African Americans. (Courtesy Colorado Historical Society)

southern lands explored by the likes of Daniel Boone. After the Louisiana Purchase doubled the size of the country in 1803, the West came to include the central part of the continent, called the "Great American Desert" until its potential for agricultural bounty was discovered in the 1850s. During the 1840s an agreement with Britain gained the southern part of Oregon Territory (later Oregon, Washington state, and Idaho), and conquests from Mexico added Texas, California, and the land that would become Arizona, Nevada, Utah, and parts of Colorado, New Mexico, and Wyoming. By the end of the decade, the western frontier of the United States stretched to the Pacific Ocean.

African Americans took part in all stages of the westward movement, which first became substantial in the 1830s. Relatively few blacks, however, crossed the Mississippi before the Civil War began in 1861. There was little work in most parts of the West either to attract free blacks or to give slaveowners a reason to bring their valuable property to places where the risk of losing it was high. Most African Americans who went west before the war fell into three groups: They were slaves brought by southern settlers to Texas; they were nominal slaves—actually more like companions—of southern American Indians, who accompanied their "owners" when the Native Americans were forced to move to Indian Territory (later Oklahoma) in the 1820s and 1830s; or they were free blacks who came to California as part of the gold rush.

Larger numbers of African Americans moved west after the Civil War ended in 1865. Census figures showed only 7,689 blacks in western states in 1860, but by 1880 the figure had risen to 72,575. Some of these new arrivals came as cowboys, making their long trail drives north through the Midwest from Texas, or as "Buffalo Soldiers," members of the four all-black army regiments assigned to keep peace in the West. Large numbers poured into Kansas, Nebraska, and other Plains states in 1879, fleeing the intolerable conditions that African Americans faced in the South after the end of Reconstruction. They took advantage of cheap land provided by the government and of a high demand for workers to establish homesteads and even all–black towns. A second wave of African-American homesteaders joined the land rush to Oklahoma in 1889, when the former Indian Territory was opened to general settlement. By the end of the 19th century, when the West was no longer a frontier and many westerners were moving to the region's growing cities, African Americans were doing the same and establishing their own flourishing communities within the larger European-American ones.

For the most part, African Americans went west for the same reasons that European Americans did. The West offered a chance to own land, start a career, or make money that many people of both races found lacking in the well-settled, highly structured East. It symbolized the same hope that had brought settlers from all over the world to North America in the first place: a new and better life.

But African Americans had other reasons for going west as well. Slavery was illegal in most western territories and

Growth of the United States

☐ 1787 U.S. Territory	▨ 1819 Florida Purchase from Spain	▨ 1846 Oregon Territory by treaty with Great Britian	■ 1853 Gadsden Purchase from Mexico
▦ 1803 Louisiana Purchase from France	■ 1845 Texas Annexation	▥ 1848 Mexican Cession	

Waves of explorers, pioneers, settlers, and others slowly pushed the western frontier of the United States toward the Pacific Ocean during the 19th century. African Americans played a significant part in all stages of the claiming and settling of the West.

states during the pre–Civil War years. Some enslaved African Americans fled to the West hoping to find freedom. A far greater proportion of the African Americans who came to the West were technically free but were limited to a lowly place in society by the segregation and discrimination that prevailed even in the North. They hoped to find a place where they would be judged on their merits rather than the color of their skin.

African-American hopes for a better life in the West were often dashed. European-American settlers who went west brought prejudiced attitudes, customs, and laws with them. Before the Civil War, both state and national fugitive slave laws required the return of any slave who escaped to the West. Slaves such as Dred Scott, brought to "free" western territories or states by their masters, learned the hard way that this freedom did not apply to them; living in a place where slavery was illegal did not set them free. They still had "no rights which a white man was bound to respect."

Free blacks learned just as quickly that they were not welcome in most western territories. They discovered that the people of the territories had outlawed slavery, not because they thought it was evil, but because they did not want to share the new land with African Americans of any status. Many western territories and states passed laws barring blacks from setting up residence, or laws that required them to post a money bond that few could afford. "Black laws" forbade African Americans in most parts of the West from voting, testifying in court, or serving on a jury or in a militia. Some of these laws remained in effect long after the Civil War. Even when laws did not

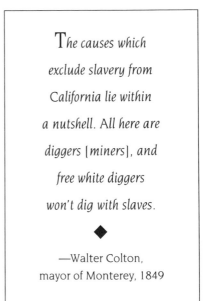

The causes which exclude slavery from California lie within a nutshell. All here are diggers [miners], and free white diggers won't dig with slaves.

◆

—Walter Colton, mayor of Monterey, 1849

prohibit black advancement, custom—sometimes backed by violence—usually did. African Americans were often restricted to separate, almost always inferior, schools, restaurants, railroad cars, theater seats, and even telephone booths (in Oklahoma).

Nonetheless, western laws and customs were by no means as rigid as those of the South, or even the North, during the same period. Especially during the early days of western settlement, there were too few African Americans on the frontier for European-American settlers to see them as threats to their jobs or their social order. Even more important, most western settlers of all races were too concerned with survival to have much time for prejudice. People who worked hard and skillfully were likely to be respected, whatever their skin color. European Americans in the West seldom treated African Americans as equals, but African Americans had chances to advance in the West that they rarely had in the East.

Segregation and discrimination, both formal and informal, became more common as the numbers of both European Americans and African Americans in the West increased after the Civil War. African Americans responded by supporting each other, forming their own social groups and organizations. From Kansas to California they founded all-black towns and settlements. Within western cities they formed church groups, literary societies, and business organizations. Individually and in groups, they fought in courts and voting booths for their civil rights. Slowly they made their way into the mainstream of western society.

NOTES

p. 2 "central and determining . . ." Quoted in William Loren Katz, *Black Indians: A Hidden Heritage* (New York: Atheneum, 1986), p. 16.

p. 2 "what is surprising and significant . . ." Kenneth Wiggins Porter, *The Negro on the American Frontier* (New York: Arno Press and the New York Times, 1971), p. 4.

p. 3 "The . . . Negroes who were brought here . . ." James Truslow Adams, *The American: The Making of a New Man* (New York, 1943), quoted in Porter, xi.

p. 7 "no rights which a white man . . ." Supreme Court Chief Justice Roger B. Taney, in majority opinion on *Dred Scott* decision, 1857, quoted in Dierdre Mullane, ed., *Crossing the Danger Water: Three Hundred Years of African-American Writing* (New York: Doubleday, 1993), p. 132.

p. 7 "The causes which exclude . . ." Quoted in Jo Ann Levy, *They Saw the Elephant: Women in the California Gold Rush* (Norman: University of Oklahoma Press, 1992), p. 210.

2

"As Cunning as the Prairie Wolf": Explorers, 1492–1860

Africans may have reached the "New World" of the Americas even before Europeans did. According to an Italian historian named Peter Martyr, the Spanish explorer Vasco Nuñez de Balboa found blacks already living in Darien, on the Atlantic shore of Panama, when he arrived there in 1513. They are thought to have been African pirates whose ship had been wrecked on the coast. Huge stone heads carved by the Olmecs, a people who lived in southeastern Mexico between about 1000 B.C. and A.D. 1100, have strikingly African-looking features. Some archaeologists, such as Ivan Van Sertima of Rutgers University, think this means that ships from Africa may have washed up in the Americas long ago.

When the first Europeans began to explore the Americas, people of African descent came with them. Some were slaves, but others were free men. Pedro Alonzo Niño, a navigator who sailed with Christopher Columbus's first expedition, was of African descent. In 1493, Columbus brought several African slaves to the island of Jamaica on his second voyage. Thirty Africans who were part of Balboa's expedition helped to build the first nonnative ships on the western coast of the American continent. Half of the 600-man expedition of Hernán Cortés, who defeated the Aztec Empire in 1519, were black. They dragged the heavy cannons that helped to terrify the Aztecs into surrender. One of these men planted the first wheat crop in the Americas.

Estevanico (Little Stephen) was the first African known by name who visited land that later became the United States. He was a slave belonging to Andres Dorantes de Carranze, a Spanish explorer. Estevanico had been born in the North African country of Morocco, in the city of Azamor, and he probably became a slave when Portugal's King Manoel captured that city in 1513.

Dorantes and Estevanico were among roughly 600 men who set out to investigate the land along the Gulf of Mexico in 1527 with Spanish explorer Pánfilo de Narváez. A combination of starvation, disease, attacks by American Indians, and other hardships wiped out most of the ex-

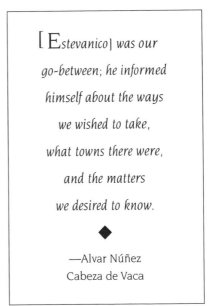

[Estevanico] was our go-between; he informed himself about the ways we wished to take, what towns there were, and the matters we desired to know.

◆

—Alvar Núñez
Cabeza de Vaca

pedition soon after it landed. Within a few months, only four men—Estevanico, Dorantes, Alonso de Castillo, and Alvar Núñez Cabeza de Vaca—were left.

The four wandered through the tropical swamps and forests, struggling to survive. Captured by Indians, they persuaded their captors to spare their lives by convincing them that they were healers or medicine men. Estevanico proved especially apt at playing this part and at learning the Indian languages.

Eight miserable years passed before the bedraggled four reached New Spain, the Spanish colony in what is now Mexico. By that time, Dorantes, Cabeza de Vaca, and Castillo had had enough of exploring and prepared to sail back to Spain. Before leaving, Dorantes sold Estevanico to New Spain's viceroy (governor), Antonio de Mendoza.

Estevanico delighted his new owner with a story that he had heard from American Indians in the Southwest during his earlier travels. Somewhere north of Mexico, the tale went, there were seven fabulous cities whose buildings were inlaid with gold and whose gates were decorated with turquoise. The Indians called them the cities of Cibola. In the Spanish imagination, they became the Seven Cities of Gold.

Eager to find these wonderful cities, Mendoza outfitted a small expedition in 1538 and appointed a priest, Father Marcos de Niza, to lead it. Estevanico went along as interpreter and guide. Some American Indians also accompanied the group as guides.

When the expedition reached what is now New Mexico, Father Niza sent Estevanico and some of the Indians to scout ahead. Niza wrote later,

> I agreed with him that if he found any knowledge of any
> people and rich country which were of great impor-
> tance, that he . . . should send me certain Indians with
> that token which we were agreed upon, to wit, that if it

were but a mean [small] thing, he should send me a white cross of one handful long; and if it were any great matter, one of two handfuls long; and if it were a country greater and better than Nueva España [Mexico], he should send me a great cross. So the said Stephen departed . . . and within four days after the messengers of Stephen returned unto me with a great cross as high as a man, and they brought me word from Stephen, that I should forthwith come away after him, for he had found people which gave him information of a very mighty province . . . the houses whereof are made of lime and stone, and are very great . . . and . . . in the gates of the principal houses there are many turquoise-stones cunningly wrought.

But then the crosses stopped coming. For days, Father de Niza waited nervously. Then, at last, two Indians who had been with Estevanico staggered back to de Niza's camp. They reported that the inhabitants of the cities had attacked their party. During the battle they had lost sight of Estevanico, but, they said, "We think they have shot him to death, as they have done all the rest which went with him, so that none are escaped but we only." Father de Niza and the rest of the group hastily returned to Mexico.

Estevanico had reached the villages, or pueblos, of the Zuñi people. These were indeed the cities of Cibola, and their multistory adobe buildings may have looked impressive from a distance—but cities of gold they were not.

Some historians have wondered whether Estevanico took advantage of the suspicious Zuñis' attack to escape to freedom. But Zuñi legends recorded hundreds of years later told of a "black Mexican, a large man, with chili lips" (that is, lips swollen as if from eating chili peppers) whom the tribe had killed long ago. Apparently Estevanico had impressed them enough to be remembered for all that time.

Estevanico's influence did not end with his death. His story of the Seven Cities of Gold inspired a second and larger exploring expedition, that of Francisco Vásquez de Coronado. Coronado and his men (some of whom were also black) traveled through land that eventually became part of Arizona, New Mexico, Texas, Colorado, Oklahoma, Arkansas, and Kansas.

The Spanish were not the only Europeans intent on "discovering" and plundering the Americas. Both the French and the British came to northern North America in search of beaver and other wild animals with valuable fur. Beaver fur was in great demand in Europe, where it was used in clothing and hats.

Some of the French fur traders were of African descent. One was Jean-Baptiste Pointe du Sable, who established a trading post [at the mouth of the Chicago River around 1779. (At that time the French and the British were struggling for control of this area, but it was ceded to the newly independent Americans in 1783.) The name of the river, like that of the major city (Chicago) that later grew up there, was a respelling of a local Indian word, *Eschikagou*, which meant "place of bad smells." Some accounts say the bad smells came from skunks, while others hold that they were from fields of wild onions that smelled bad when their flowers decayed.

Different stories are told about du Sable's background. Some historians believe that his family was French Canadian. Others say he was born on the large West Indian island of Hispaniola, in the area that later became Haiti, to a Frenchman, perhaps a ship owner, and one of his African slaves. In any case, judging from what visitors to his trading post reported of him, du Sable was a cultured man. He may have been educated in Paris.

However he came there, du Sable chose the site for his trading post well. It was the meeting point of several trails used by fur traders, yet no permanent residence had ever been built there. (The Indians of the area, who thought of all nonnatives as whites, liked to say that the first white man who settled there was black.) Du Sable's first crude log cabin

Jean-Baptiste Pointe du Sable was the first permanent nonnative settler to live at the site of Chicago. He set up a trading post on the Chicago River in 1779. (Courtesy Chicago Historical Society. Engraving by Raoul Varin, published in 1930 by A. Ackerman & Son, Inc., neg. no. ICHi-05622)

eventually grew into a prosperous settlement that included a large house, bakehouse, dairy, workshop, stable, and several other buildings. Du Sable's home, which he shared with his Potawatomi wife, Catherine, and their two children, even] boasted French furniture and a collection of 23 European paintings. In its time, his settlement was the largest and best-stocked trading post and inn between St. Louis, Missouri, and Detroit, Michigan.

In April 1803, while du Sable was still managing his trading post, the fledgling United States suddenly doubled in size when France sold it the Louisiana Territory. This immense tract of land covered most of what became the states of Montana, Wyoming, Colorado, the Dakotas, Nebraska, Kansas, Oklahoma, Minnesota, Iowa, Missouri, Arkansas, and Louisiana.

At the time this vast wilderness was purchased, the United States government had almost no idea what the land contained. President Thomas Jefferson therefore set up an expedition to find out what resources the new territory might have. He appointed his secretary, Meriwether Lewis, to head the exploring party. Lewis, in turn, chose as coleader a friend, Captain William Clark, who had had wilderness experience as a soldier.

The Lewis and Clark expedition left St. Louis on May 14, 1804. It was to travel westward, seeking a route to the Pacific Ocean along the Missouri and Columbia rivers. As they went, Lewis and Clark were to map the land, make friends with the American Indians they met, and note what useful plants and animals they found.

One of the 42 people on this history-making expedition was William Clark's personal servant, an African-American slave named York. York, who had grown up in Virginia with Clark and had accompanied him on other wilderness trips, was a powerful and impressive man. In an age when few men were over 5 feet 6, he stood more than 6 feet tall and weighed more than 200 pounds. He was an expert swimmer, hunter, and fisherman.

Even though a contemporary writer claimed that York spoke "bad French and worse English," the black man became part of the complicated chain of translation that allowed Lewis and Clark to communicate with the Indians. The only woman on the expedition, a Shoshone named Sacajawea, spoke several Native American languages and translated them to her French-Canadian husband, Toussaint Charbonneau. Charbonneau, in turn, passed the messages to York in French. Finally, York gave them to Lewis and Clark in English.

Most of the Indians who met the expedition had never seen an African American before, and Clark recorded in his journal that York fascinated them. Indeed, Clark might have been embarrassed to know that some of the Indians thought that York must be the leader of the group. One member of the Flatheads said later,

> One of the strange men was black. He had painted himself in charcoal, my people thought. In those days it was the custom for warriors . . . who had been brave and fearless, the victorious ones in battle, [to paint] themselves in charcoal [when returning home]. So the black man, [we] thought, had been the bravest of his party.

Some Indians even rubbed York's skin to see whether the "charcoal" would come off.

Clark quickly recognized York's value in impressing the Native Americans. He ordered his tall servant to perform lively dances for them. Clark wrote that this "amused the crowd very much, and somewhat astonished them, that so large a man should be active."

Far from objecting to acting as a sort of traveling circus exhibit, York seemed to have enjoyed the process—at least at first. When the expedition met the Nez Percé, he added to the show by telling them he was a wild animal that had been tamed by the Europeans. "To convince them [he] showed them feats of strength which, added to his looks, made him more terrible than we wished him to be," Clark wrote. After a while, though, York apparently tired of the game. When one Indian too many rubbed the black man's skin, York threatened the man with a knife.

The Lewis and Clark expedition reached the Pacific on November 7, 1805. Then they worked their way back to St. Louis, where they were given a heroes' welcome on September 23, 1806. According to most accounts, Clark eventually freed York, but it is not clear what happened to York after that. Clark later claimed that York started a freight line running between Richmond, Virginia, and Nashville, Tennessee, but failed at it. Clark said that York then tried to return to him but died of illness on the way. Other accounts say that York went back to the wilderness and became a fur trader or even an Indian chief.

Most of the few United States citizens who followed Lewis and Clark's footsteps west of the Mississippi in the early days of the 19th century were fur traders or "mountain men." They lived in the wilderness for most of the year, trapping animals or buying furs from the Indians. Most learned Indian languages, and many lived with Indian groups or married Native American women.

Although their numbers were small, African Americans joined in all aspects of the fur trade. They were independent trappers, voyageurs (traders), and clerks in the company trading posts. Some were personal servants to the wealthier European-American traders. Blacks were in special demand as interpreters for dealing with Native Americans.

Historians disagree about how well other fur traders treated the African Americans in their profession. Historian W. Sherman Savage says, "In most cases, the black worker was the lowest paid [of workers in the fur trade], and he was often asked to perform functions that whites refused." Kenneth Porter, however, maintains that free blacks had no more trouble advancing in the fur trade than whites did. "On the frontier the racial division lay between Indian and white rather than between white and Negro," Porter notes.

African Americans did not rise to high positions in the fur companies, and few became owners of large trading posts. There were, however, exceptions, and the Bonga family was one of them. The first of the clan, Jean Bonga, was brought to what would become Michigan as the slave of Captain Daniel Robertson, a British officer, in 1782. Bonga may have come from the West Indies or from a French settlement in Missouri. He eventually became an independent fur trader, and one of his sons, Pierre Bonga, followed in his footsteps, in what would later be Minnesota. Pierre's sons, George and Stephen, also became fur traders in Minnesota.

George Bonga spoke English, French, Chippewa (he and his father both married Chippewa women), and several other Native American languages, so it is not surprising that he also acted as an interpreter. He worked for Governor Lewis Cass of Michigan Territory and helped to draft several treaties with Indian groups. In time he and Stephen Bonga owned several trading posts. A visitor in 1856 described George Bonga as "a prominent trader and a man of wealth and consequence" and a "thorough gentleman in both feeling and deportment [behavior]." The Bonga family eventually left more than a hundred descendants. Bongo Township in Cass County, Minnesota, was named after this pioneer family.

Compared with some black mountain men, George Bonga led a settled life. More adventurous was Edward Rose, the first African American known to have traveled extensively and lived in the far West. The Native Americans called him Cut Nose because his nose had been injured in a sword fight. Rose was born in Louisville, Kentucky, and began a life of travel at age 17. He worked on the lower Mississippi for a while—as a pirate, some said. He then moved to St. Louis, the headquarters of the western fur trade.

By 1807, not long after York had passed through the country with Louis and Clark, Rose had traveled as far as the Yellowstone area and had taken up residence with the Crow people. He joined various fur trading expeditions as guide, interpreter, and hunter. He was said to speak a dozen Indian languages. Some contemporaries painted Rose as an outlaw, but H. M. Chittenden, a historian who has studied

During an adventurous life, mountain man James Beckwourth trapped beaver, led Crow warriors into battle, and discovered a pass through the Sierra Nevada.
(Courtesy Denver Public Library, Western History Department)

the fur trade extensively, writes that "everything definite that is known of him is entirely to his credit."

Whether or not they liked him, people who knew Rose usually admired him. Captain Reuben Holmes of the U.S. Army wrote of him in 1848:

> He was as cunning as the prairie wolf. He was a perfect woodsman. He could endure any kind of fatigue and privation as well as the best trained Indians. He studied men. There was nothing that an Indian could do, that Rose did not make himself master of. He knew all that Indians knew. He was a great man in his situation.

Unquestionably, the best known African-American mountain man was James Beckwourth. Beckwourth was born in Fredericksburg, Virginia, in 1798. As a teenager he went to St. Louis, the city from which most fur trading expeditions started. There Beckwourth apprenticed to a blacksmith, but he had a fight with his employer and ran away. He joined William H. Ashley's Rocky Mountain Fur Company as a horse buyer in 1824 or 1825.

After a few years of working for Ashley, Beckwourth set off on his own. He was taken into the Crow Nation after an old Crow woman hailed him as her long-lost son. At first the Crow called him Morning Star, but later, after he had led warriors to victory in many battles, they changed his name to Bloody Arm. According to Beckwourth's own account, he lived with the Crow for 11 years, married a woman named Still-Water, and became a leader of the tribe. During all this time he continued to work as a trapper and trader.

Eventually Beckwourth left the Crow and trapped his way west. He reached California in 1844. After gold was discovered in the state in 1848, he tried his hand at mining, but he quickly found that acting as a guide for incoming wagon trains was more profitable.

Jim Beckwourth
Discovers Beckwourth Pass

One of the most difficult tasks facing the pioneers who came overland to California was finding a way across the towering range of the Sierra Nevada. Jim Beckwourth, therefore, was delighted to discover a pass, or low spot, through the mountains in the northern part of the state during a prospecting trip in 1850. His account of the discovery paints a vivid picture of the beautiful valley that marked the pass.

> It was the latter end of April when we entered upon an extensive valley at the northwest extremity of the Sierra range. The valley was already robed in freshest verdure [green plant growth], contrasting most delightfully with the huge snow-clad masses of rock we had just left. Flowers of every variety and hue [color] spread their variegated charms before us; magpies were chattering, and gorgeously plumaged birds were caroling in the delights of unmolested solitude. Swarms of wild geese and ducks were swimming on the

In 1850 Beckwourth discovered a pass through the Sierra Nevada near what is now Reno, Nevada. He established a trading post on the spot and lived there for many years, guiding and trading with settlers who went that way. There, in 1855, he dictated his autobiography to a traveling journalist named Thomas Bonner. Like the autobiographies of Davy Crockett, Jim Bridger, and other explorers and mountain men of the era, Beckwourth's book contains some stories that surely must have been exaggerated, but historians have found it to be reliable in its main points. Ironically, the book does not mention that Beckwourth was mostly black, and this fact became increasingly obscured with time. In a 1951 movie, the part of Beckwourth was played by a white actor.

One story about Beckwourth's death is just as romantic as those he told about his life. In 1866 he returned to visit his old friends the Crow. Legend has it that the tribe asked surface of the cool crystal stream, which was the central fork of the Rio de las Plumas, or sailed the air in clouds over our heads. Deer and antelope filled the plains, and their boldness was conclusive that the hunter's rifle was to them unknown. Nowhere visible were any traces of the white man's approach, and it is probable that our steps were the first that ever marked the spot. . . . This, I at once saw, would afford the best wagon-road into the American Valley approached from the eastward.

Beckwourth's pass proved to be the lowest one in the Sierra Nevada. It became part of a popular wagon route into northern California and later was also used by the Western Pacific Railroad. Beckwourth established a trading post in the valley and provided accommodations, supplies, and guide service for people who used the pass. "My house is considered the emigrant's landing-place, as it is the first ranch he arrives at in the golden state, and is the only house between this point and Salt Lake," he wrote. The pass, a nearby mountain peak, and a small town—all just west of the California border near Reno—still bear Beckwourth's name.◆

him to stay with them as their chief, believing that he brought them good luck. When Beckwourth refused, they poisoned him so that his spirit, at least, would stay with them forever. The truth appears to be more prosaic: Beckwourth probably died of food poisoning before he ever reached the Crow.

The trailblazers in any country's history tend to be bold, independent, and a little larger than life. That certainly was true of African Americans such as Estevanico, York, and James Beckwourth. Whether or not they chose their exploring careers, they used intelligence, skill, and courage to make the most of them.

NOTES

p. 11 "[Estevanico] was our go-between . . . ." Quoted in William Loren Katz, *Black Indians: A Hidden History* (New York: Atheneum, 1986), p. 91.

pp. 12–13 "I agreed with him . . ." Richard Hakluyt, *Hakluyt's Collection of the Early Voyages, Travels, and Discoveries of the English Nation* (London, 1810), quoted in William Loren Katz, *Eyewitness: A Living Documentary of the African American Contribution to American History* (New York: Simon and Schuster, 1995), pp. 31–32.

p. 13 "We think they have shot him . . ." Hakluyt, quoted in Katz, *Eyewitness*, pp. 31–32.

p. 13 "black Mexican . . ." Woodbury Lowery, *The Spanish Settlements Within the Present Limits of the United States* (New York, 1901), quoted in Kenneth Wiggins Porter, *The Negro on the American Frontier* (New York: Arno Press and the New York Times, 1971), p. 11.

p. 16 "bad French . . ." Reuben Thwaites, ed., *Original Journals of the Lewis and Clark Expedition, 1804–1806* (New York, 1904), quoted in Porter, p. 13.

p. 17 "One of the strange . . ." Quoted in William Loren Katz, *The Black West* (Seattle, Wash.: Open Hand Publishing, 1987), p. 15.

p. 17 "amused the crowd . . ." Thwaites, quoted in Porter, p. 13.

p. 17 "To convince them . . ." Thwaites, quoted in Porter, p. 12.

p. 18 "The old fur traders . . ." *Ten Years' Work for Indians at Hampton Institute, Va., 1878-1888* (Hampton, Va., 1888), quoted in Porter, p. 150.

p. 18 "In most cases . . ." W. Sherman Savage, *Blacks in the West* (Westport, Conn.: Greenwood Press, 1976), p. 65.

p. 18 "On the frontier . . ." Porter, p. 146.

p. 19 "a prominent trader . . ." Quoted in Porter, p. 82.

p. 21 "everything definite . . ." Quoted in Katz, *Black West*, p. 26.

p. 21 "He was as cunning . . ." Reuben Holmes, *The Five Scalps*, quoted in Katz, *Black West*, p. 28.

pp. 22–23 "It was the latter end . . ." Thomas D. Bonner, *The Life and Adventures of James P. Beckwourth* (1856; Lincoln: University of Nebraska Press, 1972), pp. 515–516.

p. 23 "My house is considered . . ." Bonner, p. 519.

3

"Frontiersmen Par Excellence": Pioneers, 1526–1860

Most Americans have heard of Jamestown, the first permanent English settlement in what would become the United States. It was established in 1607 in territory that is now Virginia. Some have heard of St. Augustine, a Spanish settlement started in Florida in 1565. It was the first permanent European settlement in what later became the United States.

The first permanent North American settlers belonging to any nonnative group, however, took up residence almost 40 years before St. Augustine and more than 80 years before Jamestown. They were Africans.

In 1526, a year before Estevanico and his master left Spain, Lucas Vásquez de Ayllón and about 500 other Spaniards settled near the Pedee River, on the coast of what later became South Carolina. They brought with them about one hundred African slaves, the first to be taken to live in land that would later belong to the United States.

Ayllón's colony failed. All but 150 of its Spanish members died within a few months, and the survivors returned to the Spanish colony on Hispaniola. Even before the Spanish retreated, though, the African slaves had gained their freedom. They revolted against the Spanish and fled into the wilderness, joining with local Native Americans. When the Spanish left, the Africans remained.

The loss of their slaves was not the only thing that doomed the Ayllón colony, but it surely must have helped. From the beginning, Spanish and Portuguese settlements in the Americas depended heavily on the labor of African slaves. The European newcomers also tried to enslave the American Indians, but most Indian slaves either quickly died or escaped to relatives in the wilderness. The Europeans came to prefer Africans to Indians as slaves because the Africans were stronger, knew how to farm in the tropics, resisted European diseases, and, above all, had no homes or kinfolk nearby.

Between 1502 and 1600, the Spanish and Portuguese brought some 90,000 African slaves to South and Central America. A smaller number were taken to settlements in Florida, Texas, California, and other parts of southern North America. Some of these slaves helped to raise crops of tobacco, sugarcane, and indigo (a plant used to make a valuable dark blue dye used to prevent white fabrics from yellowing). Others worked in mines or waited on the Europeans. In 1537 the viceroy of New Spain asked

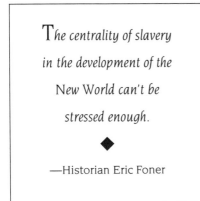

The centrality of slavery in the development of the New World can't be stressed enough.

◆

—Historian Eric Foner

the Spanish king to send more African slaves to the colony, saying that they were "indispensable for the cultivation of the land and the increase of the royal revenue."

Many of the slaves in the Spanish settlements in South-Central, and North America worked in bondage until they died—but by no means all. Like the slaves in the Ayllón colony, a number of other Africans brought to the Americas escaped into the wilderness, deciding that they would rather take their chances with alligators or jaguars than live in chains.

Especially in South America, some of these runaways, whom the Spanish called *maroons*, set up independent settlements in the rain forest. The longest-lasting maroon settlement was Palmares in Brazil, which was founded in 1607, the same year as Jamestown. It survived for 90 years and at one time had a population of 20,000.

Other African slaves joined forces with the Native Americans. The two groups had a common enemy and could help each other: the Indians knew how to survive in the local environment, and the Africans knew the Europeans' languages, weapons, habits, and weaknesses. As early as 1502 the viceroy of New Spain complained to the king about African slaves who "fled among the Indians and taught them bad customs and never would be recaptured." The chief bad custom, presumably, was active resistance to the Europeans.

As settlers from other European countries began to come to North America, they, too, brought African servants or slaves. The first Africans brought to an English colony, some 20 men and women, reached Jamestown in 1619 aboard a Dutch ship. The Dutch captain traded the Africans to the English for food and supplies.

At first, the Africans in most North American colonies were no worse off than were the colonies' poorer European residents. Unlike the Africans in Central and South America, they were not true slaves. Rather, they were indentured servants, required to work for a certain length of time but free after that. Poor Europeans often worked as indentured servants to pay the costs of coming to America as well.

Some people of African descent, in fact, became prominent citizens in the early colonies. Matthias DeSousa, for instance, was among the first settlers of the colony of Maryland. He became a well-known trader with the local Indians and in 1641 was elected to the General Assembly, the colony's governing body.

As the southern colonies began to grow more and more crops that required large numbers of field workers, such as cotton, tobacco, and indigo, wealthier colonists looked for a way to guarantee that a sufficient labor force would remain on their farms. In the 1660s several southern colonies, starting with Maryland and Virginia, passed laws that indentured people of African descent for life, in effect making them slaves. By 1790 there were nearly 700,000 slaves in the newborn United States, mostly in the South. There were far fewer in the North because farming there did not require large numbers of field hands. Most African Americans in the North either were free upon arriving in the Americas or were set free shortly after the Revolutionary War, though they were by no means treated as equals.

European settlers in North America, like those in Central and South America, feared an alliance between African Americans and Native Americans. "Their mixing is to be prevented as much as possible," one British officer advised. Nonetheless, just as had happened in Latin America—although not on as large a scale—members of the two groups did sometimes join forces. Intermarriage between blacks and Indians became so common in some places that, for example, Thomas Jefferson wrote that the Mattaponi of Virginia had "more negro than Indian blood in them." Especially along the East Coast, in the Deep South (South Carolina, Alabama, Georgia, and Florida), and in Oklahoma and Texas, many people who called themselves either blacks or Indians

Like a number of other African Americans, Diana Fletcher shared the lives of Native Americans. Fletcher lived with the Kiowa people and is shown here in Kiowa dress. (Courtesy Western History Collections, University of Oklahoma Library, Phillips Collection)

The Seminole Wars _____

In the early 1800s, the frontier in the United States lay not only west but south—in the Florida peninsula, a territory that the Spanish still controlled. Many African Americans entered this frontier and found there a freedom that did not exist in the southern states.

One of the "civilized" habits that European settlers persuaded the southeastern Indians of the so-called Five Civilized Tribes (Cherokee, Chickasaw, Choctaw, Creek, and Seminole) to adopt was the keeping of African-American slaves. Among the Indians, however, slavery was very different from what it was under European Americans. Particularly among the Seminole, a group that had split off from the Creek around 1750 and moved to Florida (*Seminole* means "seceder" or "runaway"), African "slaves" were treated almost as equals.

The Africans farmed on land belonging to the Seminole and gave the Indians a share (often quite a small one) of their crop as rent. One Indian agent (a U.S. government agent assigned to deal with Indians) wrote that "the negroes of the Seminole Indians are wholly independent . . . and are slaves but in name." Indeed, the African Americans often advised the Native Americans, especially in dealing with the European Americans.

It was little wonder, then, that many slaves in southern Georgia or South Carolina escaped across the border to northern Florida, knowing that neither the Seminole nor the Spanish would be likely to return them to the United States. Some of these African Americans joined the Seminole, while others lived independently, establishing the only North American maroon settlements. Historian Kenneth Porter has written:

> The Seminole Negroes were the Negro frontiersmen *par excellence*: runaways and rebels, settlers, town founders, military colonists, hunters, stockraisers, farmers, scouts, guides, interpreters, and, above all, fighting men.

It was little wonder, too, that southern slaveholders protested this situation, fearing not only the loss of their valuable human "property" but the possibility that these ex-slaves and their Native American friends might come back over the border and attack them. Concern about African

Americans in Florida was a major reason why the United States government pressured Spain to cede the peninsula to it, which Spain did in 1819. Even before then, while Florida was still Spanish territory, General Andrew Jackson, hero of the Battle of New Orleans and later president, ordered a raid against the Seminole and their black allies, complaining that Florida was becoming "a perpetual harbor for our slaves." This raid, in 1817, marked the beginning of the three Seminole Wars, which lasted until 1858.

The second Seminole War, which took place between 1835 and 1842, was the longest. It caused the deaths of some 1,500 U.S. soldiers, as well as uncounted civilians, and cost the country between $20 million and $40 million. It has been said to be the costliest of the many wars that the U.S. government fought against the American Indians.

The Seminole had good reason to fight: they were resisting being moved from their homes to what the government had designated as Indian Territory (what is now Oklahoma) along the "Trail of Tears" that had already claimed most of the other Five Civilized Tribes and the Africans who lived with them. The African Americans with the Seminole had just as valid a reason for fighting, for slavery, even torture and death, awaited them on the other side of the border. In 1836 General Thomas Jesup, who was in charge of the U.S. troops involved in the war, reported to his superiors in Washington, "This, you may be assured, is a negro, not an Indian war; and if it be not speedily put down, the South will feel the effects of it on their slave population before the end of the next [harvest] season."

It was put down, but not speedily and never completely. Many of the Seminole and their African allies were finally forced to move to Indian Territory, but no formal peace treaty was ever signed. The descendants of some Seminole and Africans still live in Florida and boast proudly that their peoples never surrendered.

Some of those who did move did not remain in the places they were assigned. Led by two co-chiefs, an Indian named Wild Cat and an African American named John Horse, approximately 300 Seminole and African Americans fled from Indian Territory to Mexico in 1849. The Mexican government welcomed them, giving them land in exchange for their promise to guard the border from the raids of more warlike Native Americans. Some of their descendants still live in Mexico and West Texas.◆

actually had ancestors of both races (and often of the Caucasian race as well).

Native Americans who were angry about the invasion of their land, however, often did not care whether the invaders were black or white. They attacked both equally. Similarly, African Americans often fought Native Americans to defend European settlers' homes, which by then were their homes, too. In Texas in 1840, for example, a courageous African-American cook named Jinny Anderson, armed only with a large rock, defended both her own children and those of her white mistress from Comanche raiders.

Significant numbers of European Americans first started moving west of the Mississippi in the 1830s. A small number of African Americans went, too, either voluntarily or taken by force as slaves.

Some of the earliest migrants went to Texas. African Americans had lived in this area since the days when it was controlled by the Spanish. A 1792 government census listed 1,600 citizens in Texas, of whom 450 were black. When Mexico gained its independence from Spain in 1821, Texas became part of Mexican territory. Whatever their former status, all African Americans in Texas technically became free in 1829, when the government of Mexico made slavery illegal.

Mexican society was relatively unprejudiced, and some African Americans in Mexican Texas became prosperous citizens. One was William Goings, a blacksmith who owned a large shop in the town of Nacogdoches in the 1820s and 1830s. He spoke English, Spanish, Cherokee, and several other Indian languages and was therefore highly valued as an interpreter. Texas pioneer Samuel Houston said that Goings would "not tell a lie either for the White man or the Red man."

As part of Mexico, Texas could have become a haven for slaves escaping from the United States—but that was not the way history turned out. Starting in the 1820s, pioneer statesman Stephen Austin obtained large grants of Texas land from the Mexican government and brought families from the United States to settle on it. Most of these families came from the South, and they brought their prejudice against African Americans and, often, their slaves with them. They needed the slaves to work on their farms, where they raised many of the same crops as elsewhere in the South, and on their cattle ranches. By 1834, Austin's colony in Texas had 20,000 European-American settlers and 2,000 slaves. The Mexican ban on slavery had little effect on them.

When Texas began fighting to become independent of Mexico in 1835, the first person to shed blood for that cause was an African American, Samuel McCullough, Jr. Several African Americans died during the famous Texas defense of the Alamo in 1836, along with better-known heroes such as Jim Bowie and Davy Crockett.

William Goings also fought for Texas independence. When Texas became an independent nation in 1837, however, it rewarded its African defenders by legalizing slavery and depriving free blacks of their lands and most of their civil rights. Goings and a few other prominent African Americans were excepted through a special act of the legislature, but others who had been just as loyal were not so lucky. Their situation did not improve when Texas became part of the United States in 1845.

One of the unlucky African-American Texans was Greenbury Logan, a free black man who had come to Texas in 1831. He wrote later that "I loved the country and did stay because I felt myself mower [more] a freeman than in the states." He was one of the first to sign up when the war for Texas independence began. During the fighting he was wounded so seriously that he was left permanently disabled, unable to farm the land that he owned. In spite of this—and, of course, of not being allowed to vote—he was required to pay taxes on the land.

In a poorly spelled but moving letter to the Texas legislature, Logan protested that since independence

> . . . every privileg dear to a freman is taken a way and logan liable to be imposed upon by eny that chose to doo it. no chance to collect a debt with out witness, no vote or say in eny way, yet liable for Taxes [as] eny other [person].

Logan asked to be excused from his taxes because of his war service, but his pleas were in vain.

Only a few spots in the West besides Texas and Indian Territory contained more than a handful of blacks before the Civil War. One was the area around St. Louis, Missouri, where a number of African Americans involved in the fur trade lived. Some were slaves of European-American traders, but others were free men who worked for the fur companies and traded independently. At least 1,500 African Americans were already living in Missouri when York set out from there with Lewis and Clark in 1803.

Another area with an important black population was California. Most of California's African Americans came as part of the gold rush beginning in 1849, but a few were there earlier, when the area was a Mexican or even a Spanish possession. More than half of the 44 settlers who founded the city of Los Angeles in 1781 were said to be of African or mostly African ancestry. A Spanish census recorded that 18 percent of the California population was of African descent in 1790. Some of the "first families" of Mexican California, such as that of Governor Pio Pico, were at least partly of African descent.

A few African Americans outside these Spanish and Mexican families became famous in California in the days before the gold rush. Perhaps the most notable was William Alexander Leidesdorff, who was born in the West Indies to a Danish father and an African mother. Leidesdorff sailed his schooner *Julia Ann* to San Francisco in 1841 and spent the rest of his life there.

Leidesdorff soon became a leading San Francisco citizen. A trader and shipbuilder, he owned a warehouse and lumberyard in the city and a 35,000-acre estate beside the American River. He became a member of the city council and later the city treasurer. He built San Francisco's first hotel and first school and brought the first steamship to San Francisco Bay. When Leidesdorff died in 1848, the *California Star* lamented that San Francisco had "lost its most valuable resident." Only after his death did others come to realize that this "valuable resident" was partly of African descent.

Few African Americans, either slave or free, came to other parts of the West because European-American settlers made it clear that they were not welcome there. Even Horace Greeley, whose printed cry, "Go west, young man!" became famous, stated that he did not intend his message for blacks; western territories, he said, should be "reserved for the benefit of the white Caucasian race."

"Black laws" in most western states and territories severely limited African Americans' rights or sought to exclude them entirely. Several states and territories, including Oregon, passed laws forbidding blacks to take up residence in their land. States that did not go quite this far often required African-American settlers to post bonds or pay poll taxes. Iowa, for instance, required blacks who wished to live in the state to produce both a court-authenticated certificate of freedom and a bond of $500, an amount few could afford. Other black laws restricted

T*he prejudice of race appears to be stronger in the states which have abolished slavery than in those where it still exists; and nowhere is it so important as in those states where servitude never has been known.*

◆

—Alexis de Tocqueville,
Democracy in America, 1835

African Americans from voting, testifying in court, or serving in militias.

The black anti-immigration law in Oregon Territory made a trailblazer out of one would-be settler, George Washington Bush, and indirectly affected U.S. history. Before 1846, this territory included present-day Oregon, Washington, Idaho, and British Columbia. Both the United States and Great Britain claimed the territory and had citizens living there. By informal agreement, the United States controlled the southern part of the territory, primarily what is now the state of Oregon, and the British controlled the rest.

Bush, a free black man born in Pennsylvania, had lived in Tennessee, Illinois, and Missouri. In the latter state he made considerable money selling cattle before being driven out in

George Washington Bush became a pioneer farmer in the Columbia River valley after a "black law" forbade him to settle in Oregon. This picture shows the home and family of Bush's son, William Owen Bush, who served in the Washington state legislature in the early 1890s. (Courtesy Washington State Capital Museum)

1844 by a new law that banned free blacks. A man who met Bush in Missouri noted that "not many men of color left a slave state so well to do, and so generally respected."

Bush and his family came to Oregon by wagon train in 1844 with an Irishman, Michael Simmons, and several other European-American partners. Simmons and the others in Bush's group treated him as an equal and a friend. When told that Bush would not be allowed to remain in Oregon, they refused to stay there as well.

The group pushed north into what is now Washington State. No laws barred their settlement in this British-controlled area. They set up farms near Puget Sound, and Simmons also established a settlement called Tumwater. When the United States and Britain agreed to divide Oregon Territory at the 49th parallel in 1846, the United States claim to the Columbia River valley was based partly on the existence of the farms of these two citizens that it had driven out.

All this victory did for George Bush was make him once again subject to the repressive Oregon Territory law that had driven him northward in the first place. Fortunately, however, Michael Simmons was elected to the territorial legislature in 1854. He managed to get Bush and his farm exempted from the law.

Bush's farm prospered, and it continued to do so when his son William Owen Bush took it over. In addition to being so well known as a farmer that a sample of one of his wheat crops was placed in the Smithsonian Institution, William Bush was twice elected to the Washington state legislature in the early 1890s. Like other black pioneer settlers in the West, whether slave or free, he and his father showed bravery and determination in making homes in a new and untamed land.

NOTES

p. 26 "The centrality . . ." "Slavery: How It Built the New World," *Newsweek*, special issue, Fall-Winter 1991, p. 67.

p. 27 "indispensable for the cultivation . . ." Quoted in William Loren Katz, *The Black West* (Seattle, Wash.: Open Hand Publishing, 1987), p. 2.

p. 27 "fled among the Indians . . ." Quoted in William Loren Katz, *Eyewitness: A Living Documentary of the African American Contribution to American History* (New York: Simon and Schuster, 1995), p. 24.

p. 28 "Their mixing is to be prevented . . ." Quoted in Katz, *Black West*, p. 36.

p. 28 "more Negro than Indian . . ." Quoted in William Loren Katz, *Black Indians: A Hidden Heritage* (New York: Atheneum, 1986), p. 109

p. 30 "the negroes of the Seminole Indians . . ." Quoted in Scott Thybony, "Against All Odds, Black Seminoles Won Their Freedom," *Smithsonian*, August 1991, p. 93.

p. 30 "The Seminole Negroes . . ." Kenneth Wiggins Porter, *The Negro on the American Frontier* (New York: Arno Press and the New York Times, 1971), p. xiii.

p. 31 "a perpetual harbor . . ." Quoted in Katz, *Eyewitness*, p. 79.

p. 31 "This, you may be assured . . ." *Executive Documents*, 25th Congress, 2nd Session, 1837–38, quoted in Porter, p. 62.

p. 32 "not tell a lie . . ." Quoted in William Loren Katz, *Black People Who Made the Old West* (Trenton, N.J.: African World Press, 1992), p. 47.

p. 33 "I loved the country . . ." Harold Schoen, "The Free Negro in the Republic of Texas," Part IV, *Southwestern Historical Quarterly* 41 (July 1937), quoted in Katz, *Eyewitness*, p. 94.

p. 34 "every privileg . . ." Schoen, quoted in Katz, *Eyewitness*, p. 94.

p. 35 "lost its most valuable . . ." *California Star*, May 20, 1848, quoted in Rudolph M. Lapp, *Blacks in Gold Rush California* (New Haven, Conn.: Yale University Press, 1977), p. 11.

p. 35 "reserved for the benefit . . ." Quoted in Katz, *Black West*, p. 52.

p. 35 "The prejudice of race . . ." Quoted in Katz, *Black West*, p. 36.

p. 37 "not many men . . ." John Minton, "Reminiscences of Experiences on the Oregon Trail in 1844," *The Quarterly of the Oregon Historical Society* 21 (September 1901), quoted in Katz, *Eyewitness*, p. 95.

4

"Bravely Pushing on for California": Gold Rushers, 1849–1860

Word of the discovery of gold at Sutter's Fort, near Sacramento, California, in January 1848 swept through the East like a forest fire. Suddenly almost everyone, it seemed, wanted to pull up stakes and head for California. Never mind that they faced a harrowing three-month journey across the country by wagon train or an equally long and miserable sea trip. It would all be worth while if they found the wealth that they were sure was waiting for them.

Free African Americans were no more immune to "gold fever" than anyone else. They came to California hoping to find a fortune and, perhaps, fewer hindrances to advancing in society than existed in the East. African Americans made up only about 1 percent of gold rush–era California's population, but, partly because they concentrated in cities, their effect was proportionally greater than their numbers. Gold rushers also made up a substantial segment of the blacks who moved to the West before the Civil War: of the 2,179 African Americans recorded as living in Western states (excluding Texas) in 1850, the year California became a state, almost half—962—were living in California. By 1852 that number had more than doubled, growing to over 2,000. Perhaps most important, as historian Rudolph M. Lapp points out, the black gold rushers were the first large group of African Americans who voluntarily migrated within the country, not *from* something (slavery or the threat of being enslaved) but *to* something.

California hardly welcomed blacks with open arms. The legislators at the state constitutional convention in 1849 voted to outlaw slavery, but Walter Colton, the mayor of Monterey (where the convention was held) explained why:

> The causes which exclude slavery from California lie within a nutshell. All here are diggers [miners], and free white diggers won't dig with slaves. . . . They won't degrade their calling by associating it with slave labor. . . . They have nothing to do with slavery in the abstract. . . . Not one in ten cares a button for abolition [banning of slavery].

The legislators at the convention were just as concerned about "idle, thriftless free Negroes" as about slaves. They almost passed a law that, like the one in Oregon Territory, would have banned African Americans from the state. The black anti-immigration law was rejected only after long debate and at least partly because the delegates feared that including such a law might make Congress reject their constitution. Bills proposing similar laws were introduced in the state legislature several times during the 1850s. There was always a threat that one of these bills would pass—most likely depriving black Californians of their hard-won property as well as forcing them out of the state.

Black newspapers in the East, such as Frederick Douglass's *North Star*, warned African Americans of the prejudice that they were likely to meet in California. The newspapers' editorials at first advised readers against going to the "golden state." They had to admit, however, that the prospects were not entirely gloomy. The anti-immigration law might have come close to passage, but it ultimately had failed, whereas such laws did exist in a number of the other possible places to which blacks might migrate. Unlike many other states and territories, California had few laws that prevented African Americans from gaining property or advancing economically. It might not offer blacks as many rights as they had in the Northeast, but it offered them more than they had in the South, and it had a less rigid social structure than any eastern state.

And finally, there were the gold rush success stories —which the papers also printed. "A darkey [in California] is just as good as a polished gentleman and can make more money," one perhaps overenthusiastic new Californian wrote. Readers worried about struggling to survive on their own were reassured to read that some of the early arrivals in San Francisco had formed a mutual aid society to help newcomers. Ultimately, as Rudolph Lapp writes, "Blacks, like whites, saw what they wanted to see." By the end of 1849, even Frederick Douglass had changed his mind and was urging African Americans to give California a try.

Free African Americans who reached northern California's mining camps never knew what to expect. If they met unprejudiced miners from New England or the British Isles, they might be allowed to dig or pan for gold alongside the

European Americans or even form partnerships with them. More commonly, they worked separately from the whites but were not harassed. If the European Americans they encountered were from the South, however, blacks miners might find their claims stolen or their shacks burned.

Black slaves—and the few masters who brought them—usually received an even cooler welcome. When a Texas family brought 15 slaves to a mining camp called Rose's Bar in 1850, for example, the other miners insisted that they leave the area at once. In addition to feeling that working next to slaves was "degrading," white miners had no desire to compete with a labor force that did not have to be paid.

European-American miners' mixed feelings about blacks were heightened by a popular belief that African Americans were lucky at finding gold. People told stories such as that of a black man named Livingston, who came to a camp called Mokelumne Hill in 1851. European-American miners who were there before him forced Livingston to stake his claim on what they thought was the worst spot in the area. Livingston promptly made a major gold strike there. Another story told of a white prospector who struck it rich after his slave dreamed that he found gold underneath their cabin. The prospector dug, and there the yellow metal was.

Although they sometimes encountered prejudiced treatment and violence, African Americans in California stood a better chance of being accepted on their merits in mining camps than they did in the cities, where society was more rigidly stratified. In either place, furthermore, they were likely to be treated better than Native Americans or Chinese

This black miner was one of more than a thousand African Americans who joined the California gold rush. (Courtesy Bancroft Library, University of California, Berkeley)

were. European Americans in California were more likely to fear (and therefore mistreat) Chinese than they were blacks because there were far more Chinese: in 1852, California had about 2,000 blacks and 17,000 Chinese. The Chinese, therefore, were much more significant rivals for mining claims and jobs. African Americans and Chinese, by contrast, generally got along well with each other. In most instances African Americans also had amiable relationships with the state's other two minority groups, Indians and Mexicans.

Most African Americans who came to California in the first years of the gold rush tried their luck in the gold fields. Some, however, like people of other races who arrived during this era, found that "mining the miners"—making money from the businesses that sprang up to serve those looking for gold—was more profitable than panning in riverbeds or digging holes in the ground. They moved to northern California's growing cities and took jobs there. Almost half of the African Americans in gold rush California lived and worked in cities, especially San Francisco and Sacramento. Two smaller northern California cities, Stockton and Marysville, also had significant numbers of blacks.

Segregation in these cities was neither strict nor enforced by law. It was least pronounced at either end of the social scale. Whites, blacks, and Latin Americans who could afford nothing better lived more or less side by side in the poorer and older parts of town. At the other extreme, a small number of well-to-do African-American families lived among the equally affluent European Americans in San Francisco's newer districts. Working-class and middle-class blacks tended to cluster together, usually along the cities' waterfronts because many of the men worked on ships.

Barred from some of the city's organizations, such as private libraries, African Americans set up their own equivalents. For instance, in 1853 San Francisco blacks established the San Francisco Atheneum. It had a saloon on the ground floor and a library and meeting hall on the second floor. Black community leaders met there to discuss ways to fight for their people's civil rights.

City schools, too, tended to be segregated, though the law left the matter up to individual school boards. As the San Francisco *Daily Evening Bulletin* noted in the 1850s:

> We hold it to be wise and true policy to maintain the social distinctions between the white and inferior races in our State. . . . Nothing could possibly have so powerful an effect in destroying these prejudices as educating the two races together; for if children are taught together and allowed to play promiscuously [without restraint], the whites will lose their natural repulsion to blacks, and grow up with a feeling of equality and fraternization.

African-American elementary students in San Francisco in the 1850s and early 1860s went to school in the basement of a black church, St. Cyprian's. In 1862 their parents, petitioning the city board of education for a new school, complained that

> the room in which [the children] are taught . . . is badly ventilated—the air from the west and north sides comes laden with the effluvia [waste gas] of cellars, sinks and vaults contiguous [adjoining], and is foul and unhealthful.
>
> The hall above the school-room is occupied by a military company. The loud sounds arising from their exercises, at times, greatly disturb those of the schoolroom. The plastering is broken and falling from the ceiling, so that the water from above runs through the floor upon the desks and floor of the schoolroom beneath.

The children finally got a new school in 1864. According to the school superintendent, it was "comfortable and neat"—but it was still segregated.

African Americans in California cities and towns worked at a variety of jobs. Black cooks, especially, were much in demand. "A Negro cook is one of the most independent men alive," noted a contemporary, Leonard Kip. "Being a rather scarce article, he can act pretty much as he pleases." Laundry services offered another good way for African Americans to make money. African Americans also worked on coastal steamers or other ships, cut hair, or ran boarding houses. As Rudolph Lapp has put it:

> A ship's passenger, arriving at Clark's Point on the [San Francisco] Bay, might have been met by a launch owned by a black man offering to take him and his luggage to the shore. On shore he could have encountered another black, who would offer to carry his luggage to his destination in town. When he wished to dine, he could have gone to black Uncle Peter's place on Pacific and

Powell Streets. . . . If the traveler wanted a haircut, there were many black barbers to serve him. . . . Had the new arrival . . . come on a public holiday, he would have seen a black bell–ringer shouting the news of a bull fight scheduled to enliven the . . . occasion.

Some African Americans went into retail businesses. The Atheneum Institute reported in 1854 that blacks in San Francisco owned, among other things, four boot and shoe stores, four clothing stores, eight delivery wagons, two furniture stores, 12 saloons, two restaurants, 16 barbershops, one library, and one brass band.

Some black businessmen became quite wealthy. One was Mifflin W. Gibbs, who ran a clothing store and a shoe store in San Francisco. Gibbs once said, "Fortune . . . seldom fails to surrender to pluck, tenacity, and perseverance," and he certainly found this true in his own life.

As a young man in Philadelphia, Gibbs had been active in the movement to abolish slavery and in the Underground Railroad, the secret network that helped slaves escape. After coming to California in 1850, he became a leader in the movement to fight for African-American civil rights that began there during the gold rush. He was the editor of the West's first African-American newspaper, *The Mirror of the Times*, which began being published in 1856. Gibbs was typical of the active, articulate men and women who led San Francisco's African-American community.

In a personal protest against injustice, Gibbs once refused to pay a poll tax during the 1850s. He explained that because he was not allowed to vote, he should not be required to pay the tax. The state promptly seized a large quantity of goods from his store and proceeded to auction them off to get its money. At the auction, fortunately, Gibbs's friends moved through the crowd, telling people why the goods had been seized and urging them not to bid. Everyone complied, and Gibbs got his property back. Although the poll tax remained on the law books, Gibbs said in his autobiography that no further attempts were made to collect from African Americans.

Gibbs, and Jeremiah B. Sanderson, William H. Yates, and other leaders of California's African-American community held statewide "colored conventions" in 1855, 1856, and 1857 to discuss ways of fighting state laws that limited blacks' civil rights. The first two conventions were held in Sacramento and the third in San Francisco. Most of the convention delegates came from these two cities.

The California leaders modeled their conventions after state and national black conventions in the Northeast. Their call to the first convention was aimed especially at free African Americans who came from that area and had been disappointed at the way they were treated in California:

> Brethren—your state and condition in California is one of social and political degradation; one that is unbecoming a free and enlightened people. Since you have left your friends and peaceful homes in the Atlantic States, and migrated to the shores of the Pacific, with hopes of bettering your condition, you have met with one continuous series of outrages, injustices, and . . . wrongs, unparalleled in the history of nations.

Unlike eastern colored conventions, the three California conventions spent little time discussing national issues such as slavery and possible emigration to other countries. Instead, they focused on issues within the state. Their chief concern was the state law, passed in 1850, that forbade African Americans from testifying in court in any case that involved European Americans.

California blacks were particularly concerned about this law because the crime rate was rising, especially in San Francisco, and many blacks in the cities had accumulated substantial property that they wanted to protect. (The 1855 convention claimed that 4,815 African Americans in Cali-

"Colored Conventions" and the Emigration Question____

"Organize, organize, and organize." African Americans knew that this command offered their only hope for directly combating both slavery and the oppressive laws that limited black civil rights in the supposedly free North and West. In the early 19th century, therefore, they began to call state and national "colored conventions" to discuss ways of fighting for their rights through the legislatures and courts. The men and women who attended these conventions were among the most educated and politically active members of the African-American community. Their leaders were men like Frederick Douglass, who, if they had been born with a different skin color, probably would have risen to high office in the nation.

The first known colored convention was called by black leaders in Philadelphia in 1817 to protest the organization of the American Colonization Society. This group was controlled by European Americans, many of them slave owners, who wanted to "help" slaves by sending them back to Africa. Many African Americans opposed this movement,

fornia owned a total of $2,413,000 in real estate and personal property, making them America's wealthiest black community.) They knew that if they could not be witnesses in court, crimes committed against them would not be punished.

Mifflin Gibbs and his business partner, Peter Lester, had had personal experience with this problem. One day in 1851, two white men had entered their shoe store. One man tried on a pair of boots and asked that they be held for him to pick up later. A little while afterward, the second man came back and asked to try on the boots that his friend had left. Once the boots were on his feet, he walked out the door. Still later, both men came back; the first man demanded his boots, and, when they could not be produced, beat Lester with his walking stick. Lester did not dare to fight back. Because he and Gibbs, both African Americans, were the only witnesses pointing out that most blacks of their time had never seen Africa and would have no idea how to survive there.

Emigration—if not to Africa, then perhaps to Canada, Mexico, or the West Indies—remained an important issue in later colored conventions as well. Some African Americans felt that blacks' only hope for living relatively free of racism lay in leaving the United States. Others felt that conditions would improve if they stayed and fought oppression rather than running from it. Emigration to the West was often proposed as an alternative to leaving the country.

Colored conventions were held often from 1830 to the 1850s, both in the eastern free states and in such northwestern states as Michigan, Ohio, and Illinois. Although both slavery and emigration were popular subjects of discussion, most talk at the conventions focused on ways to challenge or repeal the "black laws" that denied African Americans their basic civil rights. As a speaker at a convention held in Michigan in 1835 put it, African Americans were "an oppressed people wishing to be free . . . and by our correct, upright and manly stand in the defense of our liberties, [to] prove to our oppressors, and the world, that we are determined to be free."◆

to the events and could not testify against European Americans in court, they could not charge the men with either the beating or the theft of the boots.

The convention delegates decided that the best way to fight the anti-testimony law was to collect signatures on petitions requesting a change in the law and present the petitions to the state legislature. They hoped that if enough people, especially enough prominent European Americans, signed the petitions, the legislature would heed them. This tactic had already been tried, beginning in 1852, but the convention leaders hoped that persistence, combined with slowly growing white support, would eventually carry the day.

It did—but only after a very uphill battle. At first the petitions, presented by white legislators who supported the African Americans' demands, were not even officially received by the legislature. As Mifflin Gibbs noted in his autobiography, "We had friends to offer them and foes to move they be thrown out the window." Even when the petitions were received, the legislators took no action.

European-American support for changing the law slowly grew, though not always for unselfish reasons. Many whites heeded the argument that if an African American was the only witness to a robbery or assault on a European American, the anti-testimony law would guarantee that the criminal went unpunished. By 1857, Rudolph Lapp writes, "In San Francisco, the petition lists read like a 'who's who' of prominent businessmen and attorneys of the period."

The hated law was finally modified in 1863 to allow black testimony, though it still excluded that of American Indians and Chinese. Long before then, however, California's African-American community was distracted from its campaign against the law by an even greater threat. In 1857 and 1858, when unemployment among European Americans was unusually high, chances again seemed good that the state legislature would pass a law barring African Americans from California. Many of the state's African Americans were so angry about this possibility that they prepared to move out of the country, either to Mexico or to Canada. Leaders of the emigration movement announced that California's African Americans "will not be degraded by the enactment of such an unjust and unnecessary law."

When word of new gold discoveries along the Fraser River in British Columbia reached San Francisco, hope was added to fear as a reason for emigration, and hundreds of African Americans moved from California to Canada in 1858. Mifflin Gibbs and Peter Lester were among them. Lester and his family remained

> When will the people of this state learn that justice to the colored man is justice to themselves?
>
> ◆
>
> —Delegate to the 1856 California "colored convention"

in Canada, but Gibbs returned to the United States in 1869 and eventually became, among other things, the first elected African-American judge in the United States and the consul to Madagascar. A number of the other California emigrants also returned after the Civil War.

California was by no means emptied of blacks by the emigration to the Fraser River: more than 4,000 African Americans remained in the state. Their courage in toughing out the difficult times was rewarded when the anti-immigration bill again failed to pass. New African-American migrants began moving into the state in the late 1850s, although not in the numbers that had come during the gold rush.

During or shortly after the Civil War, the anti-testimony law and some of the other California black laws were repealed. After that, although African Americans in the state did not exist in complete equality with European Americans, they finally were able to enjoy some of the golden promise that had drawn them to the state in the first place.

NOTES

p. 40 "The causes which . . ." Quoted in Jo Ann Levy, *They Saw the Elephant: Women in the California Gold Rush* (Norman: University of Oklahoma Press, 1992), p. 210.

p. 40 "idle, thriftless free Negroes." Delegate McCarver, quoted in William Loren Katz, *The Black West* (Seattle, Wash.: Open Hand Publishing, 1987), p. 124.

p. 41 "A darkey . . ." *New Bedford Mercury*, August 22, 1849, quoted in Rudolph M. Lapp, *Blacks in Gold Rush California* (New Haven, Conn.: Yale University Press, 1977), p. 13.

p. 41 "Blacks, like whites, saw . . ." Lapp, p. 15.

p. 42 "A Negro woman . . ." Margaret Frink, *Adventures of a Party of California Gold-Seekers* (Oakland, Ca., 1897), quoted in Lapp, p. 30.

p. 44 "We hold it to be wise . . ." *San Francisco Bulletin*, February 24, 1858, quoted in Lapp, p. 171.

p. 45 "the room in which . . ." *Appeal*, September 27, 1862, quoted in Lapp, p. 175.

p. 45 "comfortable and neat . . ." *San Francisco Municipal Report for 1863–64*, quoted in Lapp, p. 174.

p. 45 "A Negro cook . . ."Leonard Kip, *California Sketches with Recollections of the Gold Mines* (Los Angeles, 1946), quoted in Lapp, p. 78.

pp. 45–46 "A ship's passenger . . ." Lapp, pp. 95–96.

p. 46 "Fortune . . . seldom fails . . ." Mifflin Gibbs, *Shadow and Light* (Washington, D.C., 1902), quoted in Lapp, p. 16.

p. 47 "Brethren—your state . . ." *Appeal*, April 12, 1862, quoted in Lapp, p. 212.

p. 48 "Organize, organize . . ." William Lambert, *Minutes of the State Convention of the Colored Citizens of the State of Michigan*, quoted in Katz, *Black West*, p. 59.

p. 49 "an oppressed people . . ." Lambert, quoted in Katz, *Black West*, p. 59.

p. 50 "We had friends . . ." Gibbs, quoted in William Loren Katz, *Black People Who Made the Old West* (Trenton, N.J.: African World Press, 1992), p. 94.

p. 50 "In San Francisco . . ." Lapp, p. 203.

p. 50 "When will the people . . ." *Proceedings*, Second Annual Convention, 1856, quoted in Lapp, p. 203.

p. 50 "will not be degraded . . ." *Bulletin*, April 15, 1858, quoted in Lapp, p. 240.

5

"We Had Them Strong in the Spirit of Freedom": Slaves and Slave Rescuers, 1787–1865

Few people—whether they favored slavery or opposed it—expected large numbers of slaves to be taken into any part of the West except for areas close to the South, such as Texas and Missouri. The kinds of farm crops that made slavery profitable in the South would not grow in the rest of the country. Even so, disputes about whether slavery would be allowed in the West laid the deadly trail that, like a slow-burning dynamite fuse, led to the Civil War.

These disputes were much more about power and money than they were about the fate of African Americans. Possessing different cultures, values, and economies, North and South had struggled for power in the national government since the United States was founded. Their differences became greater, and the resulting power struggle more keen, as the 19th century advanced. Lacking the fertile land and mild climate of the South, the North based its economy on industry rather than farming, and industry produced a greater growth in both wealth and population. The South, tied to a farm–based economy and way of life, felt itself in danger of being overpowered.

Slavery became a symbol for this power struggle. Both northern and southern leaders recognized that newly formed western states that allowed slavery, whether or not they actually had many slaves, were likely to be controlled by people who supported the South and its culture. Those that forbade slavery, on the other hand, were more likely to sympathize with the North. Thus the question of whether slavery was to be allowed in a new state was really a question of whether that state's representatives in Congress would be added to those who voted with the North or with the South.

Because slavery was such a symbolic issue, most southerners favored it even though they owned few, if any, slaves. Of the 8 million European Americans in the South in 1860, only 384,000 owned slaves, and 300,000 of these owned fewer than 10 slaves each. Whether or not they themselves had slaves, southerners tended to feel that slavery was essential for their economy and way of life. They saw threats to ban it as unfair interference from outsiders and possibly threats to their very existence.

Similarly, laws in effect in the North showed that many northerners who wanted to abolish slavery, or at least stop its spread, did not see African Americans as equals. In the 1840s, Gerritt Smith, a New York abolitionist, noted that in most northern states,

> even the noblest black is denied that which is free to the vilest white. The omnibus [bus], the car [horse-drawn vehicle], the ballot-box, the jury box, the halls of legislation, the army, the public lands, the school, the church, the lecture room, the social circle, the table, are all either absolutely or virtually [in effect] denied to him.

The black laws in most western states suggested that many of the people who opposed slavery in those states felt exactly the same way.

The first ruling on whether slavery would be allowed in the West was the Northwest Ordinance, which the Continental Congress passed in 1787, even before the Constitution was adopted. This ordinance forbade slavery throughout the Northwest Territories, which eventually became the states of Ohio, Indiana, Illinois, Michigan, and Wisconsin. However, that did not mean that slaves who escaped to these territories would become free. Article IV of the United States Constitution, passed later that year, stated that slaves escaping from states where slavery was legal had to be returned to their owners, even if the slaves fled to states or territories that banned slavery. This law and similar ones later passed by individual states and territories were called fugitive slave laws.

In spite of the Northwest Ordinance, some of the Northwest Territories looked for ways to write slavery into their individual constitutions when they organized as states. Indiana, for instance, tried to get around the ordinance by calling slaves "indentured servants"—indentured for a term of 99 years. A debate in the early 1820s over whether to legalize slavery in Illinois, the state's governor noted prophetically, gave rise to two years of the most furious and boisterous excitement and contest that ever was visited on Illinois. Men, women and children entered the arena of party warfare and strife, and the families and neighborhoods were so divided and furious and bitter argument against one another, that it seemed a regular civil war might be the result.

The delegates at the convention that organized the United States in 1787 created what they thought was a balance of power between southern and northern states by unofficially agreeing that states south of the Mason-Dixon Line, which ran along the southern border of Pennsylvania, would be slave and those above it would be free. At that time, this gave North and South approximately equal numbers of states, which determined the number of senators each group had in Congress, and approximately equal populations, which determined the number of representatives. Later, as populations changed and new states were formed, the Ohio River was used as a dividing line.

By 1820, however, the balance was beginning to wobble. The numbers of free and slave states were still equal—11 of each—but their populations were not. The North's population had grown rapidly as its industries prospered, and it now had 5,152,000 people and 105 members in the House of Representatives (the number of representatives a state has in Congress is determined by population). The South, by contrast, had only 4,485,000 people and 81 representatives.

This inequality produced a dispute when Missouri requested statehood in 1819. Missouri lay north of the Ohio, but it had been settled mostly by people from the South, and southern crops such as corn and cotton were raised there. It therefore requested admission as a slave state. Northerners saw this as an attempt to gain voting power for the South that, in their opinion, it did not deserve.

After much debate, Congress agreed in 1820 on what became known as the Missouri Compromise. The compromise kept the numerical balance between slave and free states by admitting Missouri as a slave state and Maine as a free state. Much more important, it attempted to decide in advance the slave status of all future western states. States above latitude 36°30'—the latitude of Missouri's southern border—would be free, while those below that latitude would be slave. At the time, both North and South felt that this was a fair arrangement.

The Missouri Compromise kept the balance of power safe for almost 30 years. Trouble broke out once more, however, in 1848, when the United States took over from Mexico the land that would become California, Nevada, Utah, Arizona, and New Mexico. The vast area of Texas had been added to the southern side of the balance when it entered the Union as a slave state in 1845, but the South was still a minority in Congress. Southern States feared that the North would overwhelm them entirely unless slavery—that is, southern power—was protected in the new territories. The North, of course, had its own interests in mind and did not want to see slavery encouraged.

Once again, a compromise kept the fuse from reaching the dynamite. This one was proposed by veteran Kentucky statesman Henry Clay, known as the Great Compromiser. Clay himself owned slaves, but he opposed the extension of slavery. His Compromise of 1850 allowed California to be admitted as a free state, as it had requested, and also stated that the slave status of the other southwestern territories would not be determined in advance. In return for accepting these proposals, which favored the North, the Compromise of 1850 gave the South a more

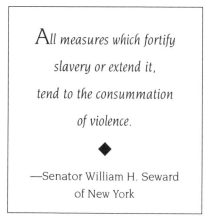

All *measures which fortify slavery or extend it, tend to the consummation of violence.*

◆

—Senator William H. Seward of New York

strictly enforced federal fugitive slave law to replace the one in the Constitution.

In response to the new fugitive slave law, the Underground Railroad stepped up its efforts to get slaves not only out of the South but out of the country. As stepping-stones to Canada by way of the Great Lakes, the network's "stations" in the old Northwest Territory states were vital in this work. Slaves usually went northeast from Ohio and Indiana to Lake Erie, or from Iowa and Illinois to Lake Michigan. Ohio alone had 1,540 Underground Railroad stations, almost as many as in all of the rest of the country. As many as 40,000 slaves may have passed through Ohio to freedom between 1830 and 1860.

As in the North, the western part of the Underground Railroad had both black and white "conductors"—those who helped the escaping slaves. John Jones, a prominent businessman who became one of the richest African Americans in the country, was an Underground Railroad leader in Chicago. Similarly, the Underground Railroad "station" —safe house or place to rest—in Detroit, Michigan, was organized by two African Americans, William Lambert and George DeBaptiste. They took fugitives to a spot near Lake Huron, where, as Lambert wrote:

> they found food and warmth, and when, as frequently happened, they were ragged and thinly clad, we gave them clothing. Our boats were concealed under the docks, and before daylight we would have everyone over [to Canada]. We never lost a man by capture at this point, so careful were we.

The free African-American community in California was also active in helping fellow blacks who were or had once been slaves. For example, Mary Ellen Pleasant, an African-American woman who came to San Francisco in the early 1850s, helped ex-slaves sent to California by the Underground Railroad by providing jobs for them in the boarding house, laundry, and other businesses she owned. When she could not employ them herself, she helped them find work in other businesses or as servants for prominent San Francisco families. Like Mifflin Gibbs and Peter Lester, Pleasant

Mary Ellen Pleasant found jobs for many African Americans in her laundry, boardinghouse, and other businesses in San Francisco. She was 87 years old when this picture was taken. (Courtesy Bancroft Library, University of California, Berkeley)

continued in California an antislavery career that had begun earlier in New England. Unlike them, she had known slavery personally as a child in the South.

Peter Lester himself invited slaves to his home and urged them to escape, explaining that they were now legally free because their owners had brought them voluntarily to a free state. (Slaves and their supporters in other free states had used this same argument to request the slaves' freedom in court, sometimes successfully and sometimes not.) "When they left," he wrote later, "we had them strong in the spirit of freedom. They were leaving [slavery] every day." A German observer of the time noted, "The wealthy California Negroes have become especially talented in such [slave] stealing. The negroes exhibit a great deal of energy and intelligence in saving their brothers."

When slaves who escaped in California were recaptured, these same African Americans, along with European-American supporters, helped them appeal their cases in court. Such appeals were far from always being successful, but several approaches worked at least some of the time. California judges sometimes freed recaptured slaves on the grounds that the slaves had not crossed state lines during their escape attempts and the national fugitive slave law therefore did not apply to them. (This argument became more difficult to use after California passed its own fugitive slave law in 1852, banning escape within the state.) The "brought voluntarily to a free state" argument suggested by Lester also worked some of the time.

In 1854 the issue of slavery flared up again at the national level, this time in the Midwest. Until the early 1850s this area had remained largely unsettled by anyone except Indians. Almost no one realized that the woodless and seemingly endless prairies, with their fields of grass higher than a person's head and their roaming herds of buffalo, were in fact wonderfully fertile farmland.

But then, as the country's population grew, so did the demand for grain crops. Inventors created new farm tools that could break up the tough soil of the prairies and make large farms efficient. Railroads began to extend from the East into the Midwest, allowing midwestern farmers to bring their crops to market quickly. Settlers began to pour onto the plains.

Very few of these new settlers were black, and even fewer were slaves. Even as late as 1860, census reports showed that only 82 blacks lived in Nebraska, and most of them were free. Nonetheless, the question of whether slavery would be allowed in this area became a burning one, just as it had earlier with Missouri and California. As in those cases, "slavery" really meant "political power." Senator David Rice Atchison of Missouri, a strong supporter of establishing slavery in Kansas, noted, "We are playing for a mighty stake; if we win, we carry slavery to the Pacific Ocean." Antislavery forces felt equally strongly, although, as before, not always because they truly opposed slavery. As one northern antislavery man who went to Kansas explained to a *New York Tribune* reporter in the 1850s:

> Many [in Kansas] who are known as Free-State men are not anti-Slavery in our Northern acceptation of the word. They are more properly negro haters, who vote Free-State to keep negroes out, free or slave; one half of them would go for Slavery if negroes were to be allowed here at all. The inherent sinfulness of slavery is not once thought of by them.

Congress worked out a third compromise to settle this new outbreak of sectional strife. The Kansas-Nebraska Act of 1854 divided the midwestern territory into two parts, Kansas and Nebraska, and stated that the settlers in each part would vote to decide whether to allow slavery there. Politicians expected that Kansas, being near the slave state

Biddy Mason Walks to Freedom _____

Biddy Mason walked all the way from Utah to southern California in 1852, breathing the dust of a 300-wagon caravan and surrounded by the lowing cattle and sheep that she and her fellow slave, Hannah, had to tend. Biddy and Hannah may have had to walk from Mississippi to Utah in much the same way the year before, when their owner, Robert Smith, brought them and their children to Salt Lake City after he joined the Mormon church. The long walks were worthwhile in the end, though, because—thanks to Biddy Mason's determination—they eventually brought the two women and their families to freedom.

As far as is known, Mason made no attempt to change her life during the four years that Robert Smith spent in the Mormon community in San Bernardino. However, during that time she apparently heard of a state law that said that slaves voluntarily taken to reside in California were

of Missouri, would vote for slavery and that Nebraska would vote against it.

That sounded fair enough, but antislavery groups were outraged because both Kansas and Nebraska were north of the Missouri Compromise line. The Kansas-Nebraska Act thus in effect repealed the Missouri Compromise. Mostly in protest against this act, antislavery groups formed a new political party, the Republicans. One of the new party's leaders was a young Illinois lawyer named Abraham Lincoln.

Offering to let people in Kansas and Nebraska choose the states' position on slavery by voting simply meant that thousands of "settlers" poured into both states who had no intention of living there. They came only to cast their votes for or against slavery in the upcoming elections. Not surprisingly, fighting broke out between proslavery and antislavery forces, and newspapers were soon carrying headlines about a mini–civil war in "Bleeding Kansas."

automatically set free. Slaves who had lived in California could not be removed from the state against their will.

Mason called on this part of the law when she learned that her restless owner was planning to move again, this time to Texas, and wanted to take her and Hannah with him. Once she was in Texas, Mason knew that she would never be free. Smith tried to take the two women and their families out of the state secretly, but Mason learned of his plan and had him arrested. When Smith's case came to trial in 1856, Los Angeles judge Benjamin Hayes ruled that Biddy, Hannah, and their children and grandchildren—14 people in all—were "entitled to their freedom and are free forever."

Biddy Mason remained in Los Angeles for the rest of her long life. She saved the money she earned as a nurse and bought land that eventually became the center of the city's business district. She used most of the money from her investments to help African Americans less fortunate than herself. When she died in 1891, the Los Angeles Times praised her "forty years of good works."◆

The group that favored slavery was victorious in the 1855 elections. Most of the proslavery voters left the state soon afterward, however, while many of the antislavery voters stayed. When a second election was held in 1856 to decide between pro- and antislavery versions of the state constitution, a majority of Kansans voted against allowing slavery.

Abolitionists might have won the day in Kansas, but African Americans and others who supported their right to freedom experienced a severe setback in 1857. Since 1846, a slave named Dred Scott had been trying to obtain freedom for himself and his family through the courts by claiming that in the 1830s and 1840s his master, an army surgeon named John Emerson, had taken him to live in several free parts

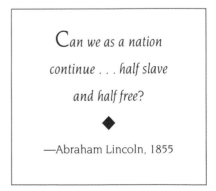

Can we as a nation continue . . . half slave and half free?

◆

—Abraham Lincoln, 1855

The 1857 U.S. Supreme Court decision that refused to give Dred Scott his freedom because his master had brought him to a free territory made "a heap o' trouble" for Scott and other slaves who had been brought to the West. (Courtesy Collection of the New-York Historical Society)

of the Northwest. By doing so, Scott's white lawyers said that Emerson had in effect freed Scott.

Scott's case eventually worked its way up to the U.S. Supreme Court. By the time the court heard the case in 1857, it had attracted national attention. People on both sides of the slavery issue realized that it affected far more than the fate of Dred Scott. If the Supreme Court ruled against Scott, it could, in effect, repeal the Missouri Compromise and make slavery legal throughout the West.

On March 6, 1857, Chief Justice Roger B. Taney handed down a devastating majority opinion. Whether free or slave, Taney said, African Americans were not citizens of the United States and thus could not sue in federal court. They were property, just like a cow or a house. As such, their owners' right to them was protected by the Fifth Amendment, which said that no one could be deprived of property without due process of law. Taking away someone's slaves simply because the person had entered a free state or territory, Taney stated, "could hardly be dignified with the name of due process of law." The Missouri Compromise was therefore unconstitutional. Most insulting of all, Taney pronounced African Americans "so far inferior that they had no rights which a white man was bound to respect."

The decision was not as hard on Dred Scott as it might have seemed. By then he had a new owner, who quietly gave him and his wife their freedom. But the case that Scott had—understandably, after over 10 years of court battles—called "a heap o' trouble" proved to be that and more for his fellow African Americans and their supporters.

Those who hated slavery swore they would not obey the ruling. Black abolitionist Robert Purvis stated that African Americans "owe no allegiance to a country which grinds us under its iron hoof and treats us like dogs." Anger over the courts's decision greatly increased support for the newborn Republican Party, and it played a major part in Abraham Lincoln's winning the presidential election in 1860. That victory, in turn, caused 11 southern states to secede from the United States and attempt to form their own nation, the Confederate States of America. The result of this seccession was a bloody civil war that began on April 12, 1861, and lasted until April 1865.

For the most part, the West was spared direct participation in the war, but men from the western states, including African

Americans, certainly fought in it. The first African Americans known to have fought in the war, in fact, were from the West. They were African-American associates of the Creek and Seminole tribes, then living in Indian Territory.

Partly because Confederate agents told them that there "ain't no more U.S.," the majority of the Five Civilized Tribes sided with the Confederacy during the war. A group of Creek, Seminole, and African Americans who had lived with them, however, refused to do so and struck out for the Union lines in Kansas. They reached them after a difficult journey, including a march through a winter blizzard.

Jim Lane, a Kansas senator, led the survivors, both Native American and African American, into Missouri to liberate other slaves there. Five years earlier, Lane, although an abolitionist, had said he thought Africans were the missing link between humans and apes. After leading the African and Indian troops, however, he called them "the finest specimens of manhood I have ever gazed upon." When African-American troops were later officially allowed to serve on the Union side, a number of other white battle leaders came to share Lane's opinion.

NOTES

p. 55 "even the noblest . . ." Quoted in William Loren Katz, *Eyewitness: A Living Documentary of the African American Contribution to American History* (New York: Simon and Schuster, 1995), p. 138.

p. 56 "gave rise to two years . . ." Governor Reynolds, quoted in William Loren Katz, *The Black West* (Seattle, Wash.: Open Hand Pub. Co., 1987), p. 86.

p. 57 "All measures . . ." Quoted in Samuel Eliot Morison, *The Oxford History of the American People*, v. 2 (New York: New American Library, 1972), p. 337.

p. 58 "they found food . . ." Quoted in Katz, *Black West*, p. 100.

p. 60 "When they left . . ." *Pennsylvania Freeman*, December 5, 1850, quoted in Rudolph M. Lapp, *Blacks in Gold Rush California* (New Haven, Conn.: Yale University Press, 1977), p. 137.

p. 60 "The wealthy California Negroes . . ." Ruth Frye Axe, ed., *Bound for Sacramento* (Claremont, Ca., 1938), quoted in Lapp, p. 137.

p. 61 "We are playing . . ." Quoted in Morison, v. 2, p. 360.

p. 61 "Many [in Kansas] who are known . . ." Quoted in Katz, *Black West*, p. 54.

p. 63 "entitled to their freedom . . ." Quoted in Jo Ann Levy, *They Saw the Elephant: Women in the California Gold Rush* (Norman: University of Oklahoma Press, 1992), p. 215.

p. 63 "forty years of good works . . ." Quoted in George F. Jackson, *Black Women Makers of History: A Portrait* (Oakland, Ca.: GRT Book Printing, 1985), p. 37.

p. 63 "Can we as a nation . . ." Quoted in Katz, *Eyewitness*, p. 187.

p. 65 "could hardly be dignified . . ." Quoted in Brian McGinty, "A Heap o' Trouble," *American History Illustrated* (May 1981), p. 39.

p. 65 "so far inferior . . ." Quoted in Dierdre Mullane, ed., *Crossing the Danger Water: Three Hundred Years of African American Writing* (New York: Doubleday, 1993), p. 132.

p. 65 "a heap o' trouble" Quoted in McGinty, p. 39.

p. 65 "owe no allegiance . . ." "Reaction to the Dred Scott Decision," *The Liberator*, April 10, 1857, quoted in Mullane, p. 138.

p. 66 "ain't no more U.S." Quoted in William Loren Katz, *Black Indians: A Hidden Heritage* (New York: Atheneum, 1986), p. 141.

p. 66 "the finest specimens . . ." Quoted in Katz, *Black Indians*, p. 143.

6

"Everything That Men Could Do They Did": Buffalo Soldiers, 1866–1898

For three decades they guarded travelers, settlers, railroad workers, and the mail from lawless attacks. They chased and often captured bandits and horse or cattle thieves. They helped to persuade the Native Americans of the Plains and the Southwest that making peace was safer than making war. At times they also protected native lands from European-American settlers. They took part in nearly 200 battles and skirmishes, and 18 of them won the Medal of Honor, the highest military award in the United States.

They also did other tasks, less exciting but equally useful. They built forts and roads, strung telegraph wires, and mapped mountains and deserts that no one other than Native Americans had ever crossed.

They were given many nicknames. The politest of those used by European Americans was "Brunettes." But the name that they themselves adopted and wore with pride was the one that came from the Native Americans, the people they fought against most often: *Buffalo Soldiers.* Some historians say the term came from the men's short, curly hair, which looked to the Plains peoples like the thick fur of the buffalo, or bison. Others say it came from the soldiers' winter coats, made from buffalo skins. Either way, the soldiers knew the name was a compliment: to Indians of the Plains, the buffalo was sacred.

The story of the Buffalo Soldiers began on July 28, 1866, a little over a year after the Civil War ended. The size of the army was being reduced for peacetime, but the government knew that soldiers were needed to protect settlers on the western frontier. While reorganizing the army on that day in July, Congress established a number of new regiments that would serve in the West. Each regiment could contain up to about 1,200 men, although in practice frontier regiments usually consisted of far fewer than that.

Four of the regiments—the 9th and 10th Cavalry (horse-mounted soldiers) and the 24th and 25th Infantry (foot soldiers)—were to be made up of African Americans. To the minds of observers not blinded by prejudice, black soldiers had proved their worth during the Civil War, in which some 180,000 had fought on the Union side and 33,380 had died. Congress voted to go on employing them in peacetime in segregated regiments.

Although all four black regiments were productive in the West, the two cavalry regiments were in battle the most and became the best known. The infantry soldiers were more apt to find themselves in the situation described by John Gregory Bourke, a western military officer:

> The poor wretch who enlisted under the vague notion that his admiring country needed his services to quell hostile Indians [would] suddenly find himself a brevet [appointed] architect, carrying a hod [tray loaded with bricks or other building supplies] and doing odd jobs.

African Americans in those days were not allowed to become commissioned officers (officers above the rank of second lieutenant), so all of the higher officers of the black regiments were white. Colonel Benjamin Grierson of Illinois was the commander of the 10th for most of its career. Grierson might have seemed an odd choice to lead a cavalry regiment because a childhood accident, in which a pony kicked him in the face, had left him both permanently scarred and afraid of horses. Nonetheless, he had become a cavalry hero in the Civil War. (He was also a former music teacher, and the 10th's regimental band was one of his pet projects.) The commander of the 9th Cavalry, Colonel Edward Hatch, had earned equal distinction while serving with the Iowa Cavalry during the war.

Both Grierson and Hatch greatly respected their black soldiers and defended them against the prejudice and indifference of government officials. From the beginning, for example, Grierson insisted that "the word 'colored' is not to be borne upon any paper relating to or connected with the regiment—its only official designation being the Tenth Regiment of Cavalry U.S. Army." (Many of the black units that fought in the Civil War had "colored" in their official name.) Their soldiers, in turn, admired Grierson and Hatch.

At first, Grierson and Hatch had some trouble recruiting officers for their regiments because many white officers refused to serve with African-American troops. They had no problem finding black recruits to sign up for the five–year tour of duty, however. The starting pay of $13 a month was not much, but it was more than most blacks could expect to make in civilian life. Army life also included free food, clothing, and shelter. With the opportunity for adventure and the possibility of partly escaping the restrictive laws and social customs of the East thrown in, it sounded like a bargain to many young African-American men.

And so they came to sign up: cooks and house painters, farmers and wagon drivers, ex-slaves and men who had been free from birth. Some were Civil War veterans; others had never been out of their plantation fields. So few could read and write that Congress assigned each black regiment's chaplain to teach the men basic literacy. Still, training slowly shaped them into a fighting force. As University of Oklahoma historian William H. Leckie has written, "In scouting, guarding, and escort duty, in the routine of garrison life, and through the iron discipline of the frontier army, pride of self and of regiment grew." That pride showed itself in the fact that the four black regiments had the lowest desertion rate in the entire army.

The African-American regiments always operated under severe handicaps. The effectiveness of cavalry regiments depended on the quality of their horses, but the 9th and 10th were given nags half-crippled by Civil War service, old age, or both. Their guns and other equipment were usually cast-offs from white regiments. Most of their diet, like that of other frontier soldiers, was a monotonous mix of beans, bread, beef, and coffee, but the black soldiers' bread was more likely than that of white units to be stale or moldy, their meat starting to spoil, and their canned food unfit to eat.

The four black regiments served mainly in Indian Territory, Texas, New Mexico, and Arizona, though they also spent time in Kansas, Nebraska, Colorado, Montana, Utah, and the Dakotas. Between 1870 and 1890, their most active years, their main task—especially that of the cavalry—was to prevent raids by warriors of the Plains Indian nations and to persuade or force these Indians to stay on their assigned reservations.

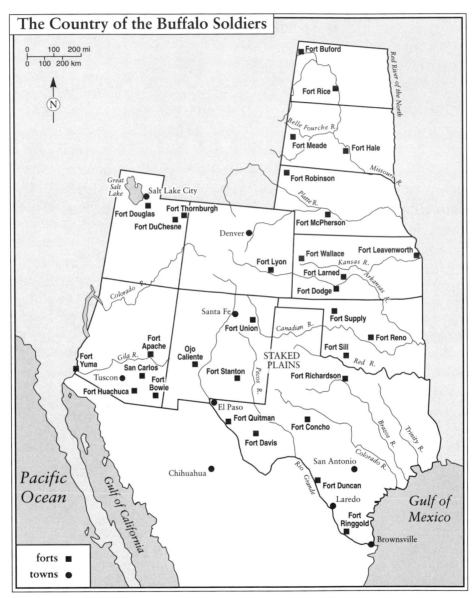

The Country of the Buffalo Soldiers

0 100 200 mi
0 100 200 km

N

Fort Buford

Red River of the North

Fort Rice

Belle Fourche R.

Fort Meade   Fort Hale

Missouri R.

Great Salt Lake

Salt Lake City

Fort Robinson

Fort Douglas   Fort Thornburgh

Platte R.

Fort DuChesne

Fort McPherson

Denver

Colorado R.

Fort Wallace   Fort Leavenworth

Fort Lyon

Kansas R.

Fort Larned

Arkansas R.

Fort Dodge

Santa Fe

Fort Union   Canadian R.   Fort Supply

Fort Reno

Fort Apache

Ojo Caliente   STAKED PLAINS   Fort Sill

Fort Yuma   Gila R.

San Carlos   Fort Stanton   Pecos R.   Red R.

Tuscon   Fort Bowie   Fort Richardson

Fort Huachuca

El Paso

Fort Quitman

Brazos R.   Trinity R.

Fort Concho

Fort Davis

Colorado R.

San Antonio

Pacific Ocean

Chihuahua

Gulf of California

Rio Grande   Fort Duncan

Laredo

Fort Ringgold

Gulf of Mexico

Brownsville

forts ■
towns ●

All-black cavalry and infantry regiments, nicknamed "Buffalo Soldiers," protected settlements in the West and Southwest, ranging from Indian Territory (later Oklahoma) to Arizona and from Texas to the Dakotas. The map shows the area and some of the forts where they served.

Forming their culture around the horse, the Plains peoples —chiefly the Lakota and Dakota (then known as the Sioux), Cheyenne, Arapaho, Kiowa, and Comanche—traditionally moved from place to place, following the huge herds of buffalo that they hunted. As settlers came and built railroads and white buffalo hunters moved onto their land, they saw their way of life threatened. The government ordered the Indians to stay on reservations assigned to them—usually only a fraction of their old hunting range—and follow a new, farm-based style of life, even though the land was often too poor to farm. Officials promised to provide food and other supplies until the Indians learned farming techniques, but the promised help often did not arrive. Faced with destruction of their cultures and sometimes outright starvation and disease as well, the Indians fought back. Both to get food and horses and to discourage settlers, they raided farms, ranches, and settlements. They sometimes killed the people they found there.

Some of the Buffalo Soldiers probably sympathized with the Native Americans. After all, their own ancestors had been deprived of their land and culture, and they or their parents often had vivid memories of mistreatment by whites. But whatever their private feelings, the Buffalo Soldiers did their duty in these wars that Major Guy Henry, a European-American officer who served with the 9th Cavalry, called "of all warfare the most dangerous, the most trying and the most thankless."

In July 1867 the 10th Cavalry was sent to Kansas and Indian Territory. Its job there was to protect farms—both of whites and of the transplanted Five Civilized Tribes—from raids and to

> We used to have a fight every day down on the Washita [River, in northeastern Texas]. A feller on the flanks nevah knew what minute he was goin' to have a horse-race back to the command with anywhere from ten to five hundred Indians a close second.
>
> ◆
>
> —Sergeant Shelvin Shropshire

Famed western artist Frederic Remington made this painting of "Buffalo Soldiers" in action. The soldiers belonged to four all-black regiments that protected western settlers between about 1870 and 1900. (Courtesy Denver Public Library, Western History Department)

guard railroad workers who were laying tracks across Kansas. The 9th Cavalry, meanwhile, went to the Rio Grande area, the border between West Texas and Mexico. Part of the 10th later served in Texas as well. Both regiments' soldiers fought bandits and cattle rustlers of all races as well as Indian raiders.

The Buffalo Soldiers faced several almost insurmountable problems in trying to control Native American and other raiders. First, there were woefully few soldiers for the size of the areas that they had to patrol. For example, at one time, a mere 4,612 soldiers had to protect 267,339 square miles of Texas frontier. In 1878 General Philip H. Sheridan, writing of the area around the Pecos River in West Texas, stated that forts staffed by a little over a hundred soldiers

are expected to hold and guard, against one of the most acute [intelligent] and wary foes in the world, a space of country that in any other land would be held by a brigade [a much larger number of men]. To do this requires sleepless watchfulness, great activity, and tireless energy.

The second problem was that laws governing where they could and could not go often kept the soldiers from doing their jobs effectively. Usually they were not allowed to follow Native Americans onto reservations without the permission of reservation agents, even if the Indians were suspected of committing or known to have committed crimes. Comanche or Kiowa raiders therefore could sweep southward from their reservations in Indian Territory, then return to the reservations when the soldiers pursued them. Similarly, the Mexican government forbade U.S. soldiers to cross into Mexico. Whenever army pursuit grew too intense, Apaches and other Indians who lived near the southern borders of Arizona, New Mexico, or west Texas simply fled into Mexico. Embroiled in its own political squabbles, Mexico seldom made any attempt to capture them.

The local tribes knew every inch of the forbidding southwestern landscape and used their knowledge to full advantage. As a result, simply finding them, never mind fighting them, was almost impossible. In 1873 Lieutenant Colonel Davidson, who commanded the 10th Cavalry for a short time, wrote that "hunting for any enemy who has the eye of a hawk and the stealth of a wolf over the arid plains and salty sandy beds of streams, I have traversed, is like hunting needles in hayricks [haystacks]."

Still, the Buffalo Soldiers' biggest challenge came not from the Indian warriors, fierce though they could be, but from the land itself. The soldiers sometimes suffered incredibly during the long scouting expeditions they had to make through craggy mountains and waterless deserts.

Some of the most harrowing of these expeditions took place in a desolate part of northwest Texas called the Staked Plains. While pursuing a Native American raiding party in 1877, 61 men from the 10th Cavalry became lost in this area and had to spend 86 hours without water. Lieutenant Charles L. Cooper, who was in charge of the group, later reported:

Black Lawmen

The Buffalo Soldiers were not the only African Americans who helped to bring peace and law to the West. A number of western marshals and their deputies were also black.

Perhaps the most famous African-American marshal was Bass Reeves. He upheld the law in Indian Territory from 1875 until the area became the state of Oklahoma, in 1907. He was one of 200 deputies hired by "hanging judge" Isaac Parker, widely known for his toughness with frontier criminals.

Reeves was famous for using detective skills and disguises, such as that of a tramp or hobo, to catch criminals, and his knowledge of Indian languages also helped him. Reeves avoided violence whenever he could, but during his career he shot and killed 14 men who, he said, drew their guns on him first. Only one of the criminals whom he pursued managed to escape him. Although he lost a coat button, a belt, and other bits of clothing to bullets, Bass Reeves was never wounded in the line of duty.

Willie Kennard was another African American who built a reputation for "getting his man." A former Buffalo Soldier from the 9th Cavalry, Kennard applied for the job of marshal in Yankee Hill, a Colorado mining camp, in 1874. To test Kennard's skills, the town mayor assigned him to arrest Barney Casewit, a gunslinger accused of rape and murder. Hardly

Our men had been dropping from their horses with exhaustion. . . . [By the third day] the men were almost completely used up, and the captain and I were not much better. . . . Their tongues and throats were swollen, and they were unable even to swallow their saliva—in fact, they had no saliva to swallow, that is if I judge of their condition from my own. . . . One of my private horses showed signs of exhaustion, staggered, and fell; so in order to relieve the men, I had his throat cut, and the blood distributed among them. The captain and I drank heartily of the steaming blood.

hiding from pursuit, Casewit was sitting calmly in the local saloon, sure that no one would dare to come after him.

Kennard marched over to make the arrest. Instead of dropping his gunbelt as ordered, Casewit tried to beat the new marshal to the draw. Before Casewit could pull the guns from his belt, however, Kennard shot first—hitting not Casewit but the cylinders of his two guns. This amazingly accurate shooting disarmed the startled outlaw and convinced the mayor that Yankee Hill had found the right marshal.◆

Marshals and deputies who brought law and order to the West came from many races. Left to right, these deputies are Amos Maytubby (Choctaw), Zek Miller (European American), Neely Factor, and Bob L. Fortune (both African American). (Courtesy Western History Collections, University of Oklahoma)

Four of the 61 men died of thirst before the group finally found water.

The main purpose of the scouting expeditions was not to fight Indian raiders but to locate and destroy their hidden camps. Loss of horses and supplies helped to force the Indian warriors to surrender and return to their reservations. Scouting expeditions also mapped the land, much of which had never been seen by anyone except Indians. For instance, an expedition led by Lieutenant Colonel William R. Shafter in 1875 discovered that the Staked Plains hid several springs as well as large tracts of fertile grassland that were ideal for cattle ranching and sheep grazing. After Shafter's report was circulated, ranchers and settlers poured into the area.

Instead of being grateful for the Buffalo Soldiers' protection, the Texas ranchers and settlers, many of whom had come from the South, often abused the soldiers because of their race. Late in January 1881, for example, Private William Watkins was singing and dancing in a saloon in San Angelo, Texas. When he became tired and decided to stop, sheep rancher Tom McCarthy, who had been enjoying the show, ordered him to continue. Watkins politely refused. McCarthy thereupon shot the unarmed trooper, killing him instantly. Post guards at nearby Fort Concho, where Watkins's comrades from the 10th Cavalry were stationed, captured McCarthy when he ran away. They made sure he stood trial, but to no avail: as usually happened when a European American killed an African American in Texas, the jury acquitted him.

In addition to the soldiers of the four regular African-American regiments, a special group of black soldiers helped to keep order on the Texas frontier. They were the Seminole-Negro Indian Scouts, the descendants of—or in some cases, the same—people who had fled to the Texas–Mexico border with Wild Cat and John Horse after the Seminole Wars. Beginning in 1870, the army recruited them to track Comanche and Apache raiders. In return, it promised them pay, food and supplies for their families, and grants of land.

The black Seminole made ideal scouts. They could speak English, Mexican Spanish, and often several Indian languages. They knew the country, they knew the ways of the other tribes, and their tracking ability seemed to border on the supernatural. General Zenas R. Bliss, commander of the 24th Infantry, called them "excellent hunters, and trailers, and brave scouts . . . splendid fighters."

Lieutenant John L. Bullis became the leader of the Seminole scouts in 1873. Bullis, a white man from New York, had already commanded black troops during and after the Civil

War. A small, wiry man, he proved as tough as the seasoned desert fighters he led.

Bullis and his scouts became true friends. He went to their weddings and the christenings of their children. The scouts, in turn, were devoted to him. Scout Joseph Phillips wrote,

> The scouts thought a lot of Bullis. . . . That fella suffer just like we-all did out in de woods. He was a good man. He was an Injun fighter. He was tuff. He didn't care how big a bunch dey was, he went into 'em every time, but he look for his men. His men was on equality, too. He didn't stand and say, "Go yonder"; he would say "Come on boys, let's go get 'em."

Three of Bullis's scouts proved their devotion on April 25, 1875. On that day Bullis and Sergeant John Ward, trumpeter Isaac Payne, and Private Pompey Factor caught up with a party of about 30 Comanche warriors leading a herd of stolen horses. The scouts dismounted and staged a surprise attack, firing from different directions to make the Comanches think that their number was larger than it really was.

The technique worked for a while, but then the Comanches caught onto the scouts' trick and began to hem in their attackers. The three scouts broke free and reached their horses, but Bullis's horse ran away, leaving him on foot among the angry Comanches. "We can't leave the lieutenant, boys," Ward shouted. Turning his horse, he dashed back into the fray with the other two scouts close behind. Comanche bullets hit Ward's rifle stock and carbine sling, but he managed to reach his commander unhurt. Then Bullis "saved [his own] hair" from scalping by leaping up onto Ward's horse. Ward and Bullis on their single mount, followed by Payne and Factor, broke through the Comanche line again and made their escape. At Bullis's urging, all three scouts received the Medal of Honor.

The government responded to the Seminole scouts' loyal and effective service by breaking almost every promise it had made to them. It had promised grants of land to the scouts and their families, but these were never given. It had promised enough food and supplies for the scouts' families as well as themselves, but around 1873 it began providing rations for the scouts only. Approximately 300 people were thus forced to live on food rations for 50. Protests by Bullis, John Horse, and even General C. C. Augur, the commander of the Department of Texas, failed to make the Washington bureaucrats change their minds. Adding insult to injury, local desperadoes and even law officers sometimes abused the black scouts.

Some scouts quit in disgust at this treatment, but others stayed on, more out of loyalty to Bullis than to the government. The group continued active duty until 1882, during which time they went on 26 expeditions and fought 12 major engagements. In spite of their fine record, the Seminole-Negro Indian Scouts received little recognition for their work. In his old age, for example, Pompey Factor, a Medal of Honor winner, could not even get an army pension.

The Buffalo Soldiers patrolled New Mexico and Arizona as well as Texas and Indian Territory. The 9th Cavalry was assigned to New Mexico in September 1875, and parts of the 10th later served there as well. The "enemy" in these southwestern territories was the Apache Nation. At first the Apache had been willing to stay on the reservations assigned to them because the reservations were part of their traditional homeland. In 1875, however, following raids by a few Chiricahua Apaches (one subgroup of the tribe), government officials decided to move all the Apaches to San Carlos, a hot, barren reservation in the Arizona desert. Many refused to go and with good reason. Even General John Pope, the army leader in charge of the area, protested that the Apache would starve if large numbers of them were forced onto this inhospitable spot. The politicians in Washington, however, would not listen.

Among the Apache leaders who refused to move to San Carlos was a powerful, clever warrior named Victorio (or Bidu-ya), the leader of what were called the Warm Springs Apache (this band included Mibreño, Mogollon, Copper Mine, Chiricahua, Mescalero, and Warm Springs Apache). For more than a year, beginning in August 1879, soldiers from the 9th and 10th Cavalry pursued Victorio and members of his band through the mountains. Victorio repeatedly surrendered on the condition that he be allowed to return to the Warm Springs or the Mescalero Reservation in New Mexico, but on being told that he would have to go to the hated San Carlos instead, he broke free again. To feed themselves, Victorio and his warriors raided settlements and

The Buffalo Soldier regiments served mostly in Indian Territory, Texas, New Mexico, and Arizona. This photograph shows men of the 10th Cavalry in camp near Chloride, New Mexico, in 1892. (Photo by Henry A. Schmidt, courtesy Museum of New Mexico, Neg. No. 58556)

ranches, often murdering any people they found as well as stealing horses, mules, and supplies. Colonel Hatch described the conditions Major Albert P. Morrow and his men faced while pursuing the Apache leader:

> The work performed by these troops is most arduous, horses worn to mere shadows, men nearly without boots, shoes and clothing. . . . In the Black Range the horses were without anything to eat five days except what they nibbled from piñon pines. . . . The Indians select mountains for their fighting ground and positions almost impregnable usually throwing up stone rifle pits where nature has not furnished them and skilfully devising loopholes. The Indians are thoroughly armed and . . . are abundantly supplied with ammunition their fire in action is incessant. . . . It is impossible to describe the exceeding roughness of such mountains as the Black Range and the San Mateo. The well known Modoc Lava Beds are a lawn compared with them.

When the soldiers came too close to Victorio's group, the Indian warrior rode across the border to safety in Mexico. At first the Mexican government did not pursue Victorio, but after repeated Apache raids on Mexican settlements it changed its policy. A three-day battle took place October 15 through 18, 1880, between Victorio's group and Mexicans and Tarahumara Indians. When it was over, Victorio was dead. The Mexican success had been made possible in part by the Buffalo Soldiers, who for months had harassed the Apache band and destroyed its camps.

In 1885, the 10th Cavalry was transferred from New Mexico to Arizona Territory, where it fought Chiricahua Apaches led by the famous war chief Geronimo. The 9th,

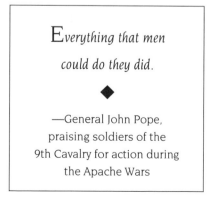

Everything that men could do they did.

◆

—General John Pope, praising soldiers of the 9th Cavalry for action during the Apache Wars meanwhile, had been sent back to Indian Territory, where the 10th had first served. There, ironically, after 15 years of fighting Native Americans to protect European Americans, the 9th found itself with the opposite job: protecting Native American land from European Americans who wanted to settle on it illegally.

The intruding settlers were called Boomers because they wanted to create a boom, or rapid growth of demand, for land in the area. Such a boom, they hoped, would force the government to take the land away from the Native Americans and open it to general settlement. Having occupied the land first, the Boomers could then make a profit by selling it to settlers who arrived later.

President Rutherford B. Hayes had ordered army units in the area to keep the Boomers out, by force if necessary, and the men of the 9th did their best to comply. Each time the Boomer wagons appeared on the wrong side of the border, the soldiers politely but firmly escorted them back to Kansas. If politeness failed to work, the soldiers increased their pressure. In August 1882, for example, they tied a group of determined homesteaders up and threw them into their own wagons like "sacks of shelled corn" before hauling them out. Since both soldiers and Boomers were armed, only luck—and the skill and patience of the African-American soldiers—kept these confrontations from turning into bloodbaths. And at that, the soldiers merely delayed the inevitable: in 1889, President Benjamin Harrison opened the land to all settlers, so in the end the Boomers won.

In 1898, during the Spanish-American War, the Buffalo Soldiers had one last chance to show their bravery. Officially this war was fought to free the large Caribbean island of Cuba and certain other territories from Spanish control, but it was also spurred by a desire to protect U.S. property holdings in Cuba and to increase the overseas territories and the power of the United States.

The most famous fighters in Cuba during the war were the Rough Riders. This group of white Americans was led by Theodore Roosevelt, an energetic young man who would one day be president of the United States. Few people who heard or read of the Rough Riders' exploits in battles such as the one fought on San Juan Hill on July 1, 1898, knew that the group owed its success—and its survival—largely to the African-American troops of the 9th and 10th Cavalry. Describing an earlier battle at Las Guásimas, Cuba, on June 24, one white officer said, "If it had not been for the Negro cavalry the Rough Riders would have been exterminated." Theodore Roosevelt himself made no secret of his admiration for the black soldiers. He wrote to a friend, "I wish no better men beside me in battle than these colored troops showed themselves to be."

The four all-black regiments were disbanded at the start of World War II. In spite of their key role in making the American West safe for settlement, the Buffalo Soldiers by that time had been all but forgotten for decades.

In the early 1990s, however, a monument to the Buffalo Soldiers, showing a black cavalryman astride a rearing horse, was erected in Fort Leavenworth, Kansas, the first home of the 10th Cavalry. The monument was the inspiration of General Colin Powell, an African American who became head of the Joint Chiefs of Staff, the highest military position in the United States. "The soldier you see here," Powell said when he dedicated the monument on July 25, 1992, "represents all of our beloved America—what we were in the past, what we are now, and, most important of all, what we must be tomorrow." Powell has called the Buffalo Soldiers "an everlasting symbol of man's ability to overcome . . . of human courage in the face of all obstacles and dangers."

NOTES

p. 70 "The poor wretch . . ." John Gregory Bourke, *On the Border with Crook* (New York, 1891), quoted in Monroe Lee Billington, *New*

Mexico's Buffalo Soldiers 1866–1900 (Niwot: University Press of Colorado, 1991), p. 28.

p. 70 "the word 'colored' . . ." Quoted in Leo W. Banks, "The Buffalo Soldiers," *Arizona Highways*, January 1995, p. 36.

p. 71 "In scouting, guarding . . ." William H. Leckie, *The Buffalo Soldiers: A Narrative of the Negro Cavalry in the West* (Norman: University of Oklahoma Press, 1967), p. 25.

p. 73 "of all warfare . . ." Quoted in Catherine Reef, *Buffalo Soldiers* (New York: Holt, 1993), p. 28.

p. 73 "We used to have a fight . . ." Quoted in Banks, p. 36.

p. 74 "are expected to hold . . ." *Executive Documents*, No. 1, Part 2, 45th Congress, 3rd Session, quoted in Leckie, p. 169.

pp. 75 "hunting for any enemy . . ." Letter to Adjutant General of Department of Texas, 1873, quoted in Leckie, p. 169.

p. 76 "Our men had been dropping . . ." *Daily Tribune*, September 8, 1877, quoted in William Loren Katz, *Eyewitness: A Living Documentary of the African American Contribution to American History* (New York: Simon and Schuster, 1995), p. 309.

p. 78 "excellent hunters . . ." Quoted in William Loren Katz, *Black People Who Made the Old West* (Trenton, N.J.: African World Press, 1992), p. 145.

p. 79 "The scouts thought a lot . . ." Quoted in Katz, *Black People*, p. 146.

p. 79 "We can't leave . . ." Quoted in Kenneth Wiggins Porter, *The Negro on the American Frontier* (New York: Arno Press and the New York Times, 1971), p. 480.

p. 79 "saved [his own] hair . . ." Quoted in William Loren Katz, *Black Indians: A Hidden Heritage* (Atheneum, 1986), p. 82.

p. 82 "The work performed . . ." Report to General John Pope, February 25, 1880, quoted in Leckie, pp. 213–214.

p. 82 "Everything that men . . ." *Annual Report of the Secretary of War for the Year 1880*, quoted in Leckie, p. 229.

p. 83 "sacks of shelled corn" Carl Coke Ricter, *Land Hunger: David L. Payne and the Oklahoma Boomers*, quoted in Leckie, p. 248.

p. 84 "If it had not been . . ." Quoted in Phillip L. Drotning, *Black Heroes in Our Nation's History* (New York: Washington Square Press, 1970), p. 139.

p. 84 "I wish no better . . ." Quoted in Richard O'Connor, "'Black Jack' of the 10th," *American Heritage*, February 1967, p. 107.

p. 84 "The soldier you see . . ." Quoted in Reef, pp. 73–74.

p. 84 "an everlasting symbol . . ." Speech given in July 1990, quoted in Reef, p. 10.

7

"An Unusually Adventurous Life": Cowboys, 1865–1905

In 1967, when historian William Loren Katz told Langston Hughes, a famous black poet, that he was preparing a book for young people about African-American history, Hughes had only one piece of advice: "Don't leave out the cowboys."

Cowboys are one of the first images likely to come to mind when people think of the settling of the West, or even of American history as a whole. The cowboy life has been celebrated and glamorized in hundreds of books, paintings, and movies. Katz believes Hughes wanted to make sure young people knew that African Americans had shared in this most American of occupations.

Hughes was right to be concerned. Many people have never heard of African-American cowboys. Wallace Ponce, the writer of a book about black cowboys, recalled that when he was a child in Iowa playing "cowboys and Indians," he and the other black children always had to be Indians because the white children they played with "firmly believed that there was no such thing as a Black cowboy."

In fact, black cowboys were common. Historian Kenneth Porter has estimated that a quarter of the approximately 35,000 men who worked in the western cattle industry between 1866 and 1895 were African Americans. Each trail crew that guided cattle on the long drives from the plains of

Two or three of the cowboys on an 11-man trail crew, responsible for herding some 2,500 cattle north to midwestern railheads from Texas, were likely to be African Americans. The cowboys in this picture worked in Wyoming in 1905. (Courtesy Wyoming Division of Cultural Resources)

Texas to rail shipment points in Kansas and other midwestern states had 11 men. Of these, two or three were likely to be black. African Americans also worked on cattle ranches, doing such jobs as taming and shoeing horses.

The trail drives that made American cowboys famous began after the Civil War ended in 1865. People in northeastern cities, who had generally preferred pork on their dinner tables in the past, changed their taste and began to demand beef instead. Large numbers of factory workers in the cities' expanding industries needed to be fed, and beef was also needed in growing settlements and on Indian reservations in the West.

The best sources of beef were the nearly 6 million longhorned cattle that roamed the plains of Texas. Those cattle were a challenge to the toughest frontiersman. Descended from animals brought to America by early Spanish settlers, they had multiplied and run wild during the war years. Before they could be used for anything, they had to be captured and branded with an owner's mark. African Americans such as Henry Beckwith were among the early cowboys who took on this dangerous work. Beckwith, nicknamed "the Coyote" by other cowboys because he hunted at night, could track cattle by smell and sound through the densest thickets.

At first there seemed no way to get the longhorns to a railroad to be shipped because there were no railroads anywhere near Texas. However, in 1867 the Kansas Pacific Railroad Company and an enterprising Illinois cattleman named Joseph G. McCoy solved this problem. They laid new railroad tracks through the Kansas prairies to the towns of Topeka and Abilene, and McCoy built pens in Abilene and urged Texas cattlemen to drive their herds to the town.

The good thing about the route from Texas to Abilene, later known as the Chisholm Trail, was that it did not pass through farmland. Cattle owners thus did not have to hear farmers' complaints about herds trampling their fields. The bad thing about the trail was that the cattle had to be driven

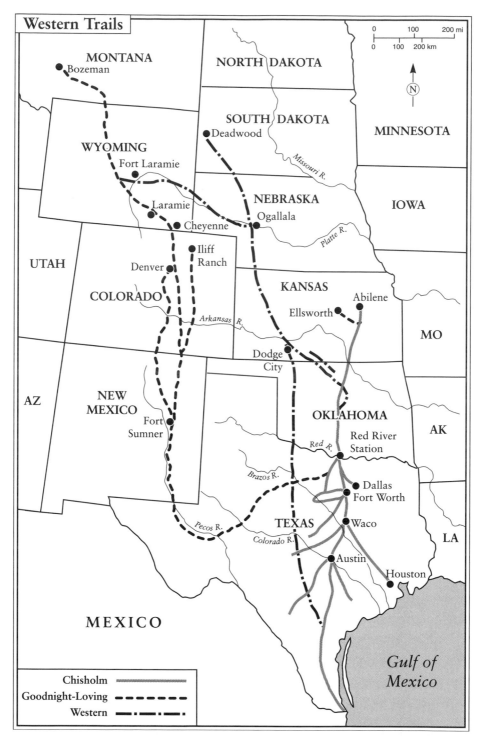

Western Trails

0   100   200 mi
0   100   200 km

N

MONTANA
Bozeman

NORTH DAKOTA

SOUTH DAKOTA
Deadwood

MINNESOTA

WYOMING
Fort Laramie

Missouri R.

Laramie

Cheyenne

NEBRASKA
Ogallala

IOWA

Platte R.

UTAH

Iliff
Ranch

Denver

COLORADO

Arkansas R.

KANSAS
Ellsworth

Abilene

MO

Dodge
City

AZ

NEW
MEXICO

Fort
Sumner

OKLAHOMA
Red River
Station

AK

Red R.

Brazos R.

Dallas
Fort Worth

Pecos R.

TEXAS

Waco

LA

Colorado R.

Austin

Houston

MEXICO

Gulf of
Mexico

Chisholm
Goodnight-Loving
Western

Cowboys drove cattle along these trails from Texas to northern pastures and railheads
in the 1870s and 1880s. Roughly a quarter of those adventurous men were African
Americans.

hundreds of miles across waterless deserts, swollen rivers, and territory belonging to Native Americans who resented the big herds' intrusion. Each trip took two to three long months. Even so, McCoy's idea caught on, and Texas long-horns were soon moving north by the hundreds of thousands.

Ranchers needed tough, experienced men to drive the cattle, and some of the best who applied for the job were African Americans. Some of these would-be cowboys had been brought to Texas as slaves before the Civil War. Others, freedmen or newly freed slaves, came west to seek work after the war was over. Both groups had often tended cattle, horses, or both as part of their former duties. Other African Americans were experienced blacksmiths or cooks. Skilled workers in all these occupations were scarce, so most ranchers were glad to hire such men regardless of their race.

Each crew on the trail drives was responsible for a herd of about 2,500 cattle. A typical trail crew consisted of the trail boss, eight cowboys, a wrangler to take care of all the men's horses, and a cook. Of the cowboys, the two most experienced rode "on point" at the front of the herd, just behind the trail boss and the cook's chuck wagon. Four more cowboys rode "on swing," at the sides. The remaining two brought up the rear, in the position called drag.

African Americans sometimes were given the least de-sirable positions on the crew, those of drag rider and wrangler. On the other hand, the cook, whose pay might equal that of a top hand (the cowboy second in rank to the trail boss), was also likely to be black. The cook's job was an important one: besides feeding everyone, he took care of the cowboys' possessions (which rode with him in the chuck wagon) and often doctored the men when they were sick. A good cook was respected and loved, and even a bad one was feared.

Most of the time, men of different races worked together on trail crews with little friction. If a man did his job well, the others respected him. Like army soldiers—but unlike people in many other occupations—black and white cowboys generally received equal pay for equal work. "The point of their history," say historians Philip Durham and Everett L. Jones in their book about black cowboys, "is not that they were different from their companions but that they were similar." A study by historian Kenneth Porter has indicated that black cowboys probably encountered less discrimination than did blacks in any other line of work open to both races at the time.

Even so, just as blacks—no matter how experienced or skilled—could not become commissioned officers in the army, racism kept most African Americans from becoming trail bosses except on all–black crews. Jim Perry, who worked as a cowboy and trail cook for more than 20 years, once said, "If it weren't for my . . . old black face, I'd have been a boss long ago." A white cowboy who rode with Perry agreed, "No doubt he would have."

There were exceptions. One was Bose Ikard, the African-American "right-hand man" for Charles Goodnight and Oliver Loving. In 1866, these two cattlemen pioneered the Goodnight-Loving Trail, one of the most heavily used routes leading from Texas to the Midwest. The trail went through New Mexico and Colorado to Cheyenne, Wyoming. When Loving died after a fight with the Comanches, Ikard continued working for Goodnight.

Ikard drove cattle on the Goodnight-Loving Trail for four years, and he and Goodnight remained friends until Ikard's death in 1929. Ikard helped Goodnight control cattle stampedes and fight off attacking outlaws and Indians. He saved Goodnight's life several times. Goodnight said Ikard

During the halcyon [best] days of the cattle range, Negroes there frequently enjoyed greater opportunities for a dignified life than anywhere else in the United States.

◆

—Kenneth Wiggins Porter, 1969

surpassed any man I had in endurance and stamina. There was a dignity, a cleanliness, and a reliability about him that was wonderful. . . . His behavior was very good in a fight, and he was probably the most devoted man to me that I ever had. I have trusted him farther than any living man. He was my detective, banker, and everything else in Colorado, New Mexico, and the other wild country I was in. . . . When we carried money I gave it to Bose, for a thief would never . . . think of looking in a Negro's bed for money.

From trail boss to wrangler, all the men on a trail crew faced hardship and danger daily. Storms and cattle stampedes were among the worst threats, and they often went together, since lightning could easily frighten the cattle. Nat Love, one of the few black cowboys who wrote about his life, described one such terrifying experience:

Imagine . . . riding your horse at the top of his speed through torrents of rain and hail, and the darkness so black we could not see our horses' heads. We were chasing an immense herd of maddened cattle which we could hear but could not see, except during the vivid flashes of lightning which furnished our only light. . . . Late the next morning, we had the herd rounded up 30 miles from where they started the night before.

At the end of the long trail drive was a cow town, such as Abilene or Dodge City. There the cowboys spent their pay on alcohol, gambling, and other amusements that relieved the boredom of weeks in the saddle. Black cowboys were much more likely to run into prejudice and segregation in the towns than they were on the trail. Racism was especially likely to surface if white women lived in the town. African Americans could usually enter gambling houses and saloons freely—though they might be served at the opposite end of the bar from European Americans—but they were likely to

Bob Lemmons, the "Mustang Stallion"

Mustangs were the descendants of horses that Spanish explorers and settlers brought to North America. (There were no horses in the Americas before the Spanish arrived.) Mustang herds had run wild on the Texas plains for centuries.

Mustangs were small, shaggy, tough, and smart. When tamed, they made wonderful cow ponies because of their speed and endurance. Cowboys and the ranchers they worked for therefore liked to capture mustang herds.

But catching these wild horses was anything but easy. A mustang herd was all mares (females) except for its leader, a strong and wily stallion. Each herd had its own territory, and the stallion knew every inch of it. To capture a herd of mustangs, cowboys on horseback—usually a pair of them—kept up with the herd until it tired, then either captured or killed the stallion. Once the herd leader was gone, the mares could be driven back to the cowboys' ranch.

find themselves barred from hotels and restaurants because women might be present in these places.

Ranch work could be just as challenging as trail drives. For example, breaking horses—familiarizing them with being ridden—was one of the hardest jobs a cowboy might do, whether the horses were colts or wild mustangs that had never been ridden or simply ranch horses that had run free during the winter and had to be accustomed to a saddle all over again. Some black cowboys made a specialty of "bronco busting" and did nothing else.

Breaking a horse proceeded in stages. First the horse had to be taught to accept having a rope thrown over its head. Then it learned to tolerate a halter called a hackamore. Next

A black cowboy named Bob Lemmons worked out a better way of catching mustangs. Unlike most mustangers, he worked alone. When he was on a herd's trail, he stayed completely away from other human beings. Other cowboys left food packages for him in trees, but he would not touch these until they had lost their human smell.

Instead of trying to keep up with a mustang herd, Lemmons followed their tracks. After a few days of following, he could recognize the tracks of "his" herd even if they crossed those of another group. He slowly worked his way closer to the herd and then rode next to them for several days. Finally the horses came to accept him.

Then Lemmons did the most amazing thing of all. He drove off the herd's stallion and returned to lead the mares himself, just as if he were a stallion. He took them to water and to new pastures. He led them out of danger, just as a stallion would have. Only when the mares trusted him completely did he begin guiding them toward the ranch.

The other cowboys at the ranch had prepared a temporary corral, or enclosure, for the horses. Lemmons galloped into the corral, and the mares trotted after him. Because he had led them in so naturally, they were not tired, frightened, or injured. As Lemmons once told an interviewer, the secret of his success was that "I acted like I was a mustang. I made the mustangs think I was one of them."◆

it had to get used to having the weight of a blanket and then a saddle on its back. Last came training with a human rider.

Of course, the horse did not want to learn any of these things. Most horses fought their trainers every inch of the way. They sometimes had to be roped, tied down, and blindfolded before a saddle could be put on their backs.

Most determinedly of all, an unbroken horse tried to throw off the weight of a rider. It might buck, twist, and "sunfish"— show its heels to the sky. The horse might jump up in the air and land stiff-legged with a bone-rattling jar, or it might try to run away from its rider or fall on him and crush him. In a week or two, though, it usually learned that the human was its master. In trying to hurt him, it hurt only itself.

Black horsebreakers often got—and sometimes volunteered for—the meanest horses, the ones the other cowboys wouldn't touch. Each bronco buster had his own favorite way of working. Richard Phillips, a modern black horsebreaker, uses a technique that the cowboys of the 1870s and 1880s may also have applied.

> Sometimes when they brought horses in for us to break, . . . we'd throw them down and tie old jeans filled with dirt on them and let them wear them for two or three days. The dirt–filled jeans would be the approximate weight of a man and the horse would buck until he got tired. A lot of times he'd buck the jeans off and we'd have to throw him again. In the meantime we'd try to . . . quiet him enough for him to get used to us.

The names of most black cowboys, even more than those of white cowboys, are lost to history. Some, indeed, were not even given the dignity of a last name, but were known simply as "Nigger Jim" or "Nigger Bob." A few, however, became famous. One who did, partly because he was not afraid to "toot his own horn," was Nat Love. In 1907 Love published his autobiography, *The Life and Adventures of Nat Love: Better Known in the Cattle Country as "Deadwood Dick."* Like James Beckwourth and other mountain men before him, and like many other cowboys, both white and black, of his own time, Love told tales about himself that could stretch his readers' powers of belief. But there is no doubt that he was an outstanding cowboy, and he certainly led, as he put it, "an unusually adventurous life."

Love was born around 1854 to slave parents in Tennessee. When his father died around the end of the Civil War, Nat, at the age of 12, became responsible for his family. To earn money for them, he learned to break colts for a neighboring rancher. He was soon able to tame a full-grown stallion.

Cowboy Nat Love led "an unusually adventurous life" and—so he said—was an expert at every skill prized on the western ranges. (Courtesy Denver Public Library, Western History Department)

In 1869, when he was 15 years old, Love won a horse in a raffle. He sold it, gave half the money to his mother, and with the other half went west to join the trail drives. He came to Dodge City, which he described as "a typical frontier city, with a great many saloons, dance halls, and gambling houses, and very little of anything else." Calling himself Red River Dick, he took a job with the Duval Ranch and rode the Kansas Trail regularly for the next three years. He then went to work for the Gallanger Company, which had a huge ranch in southern Arizona. Love worked as a cowboy for about 20 years. During that time, among other things, he learned to break mustangs, read brands (a vital skill for identifying ownership of cattle at roundups), speak fluent Spanish, and become an expert marksman.

In contests of skill with other cowboys, Love said, he almost always won. When six black and six white cowboys competed to see who could control a wild horse the most quickly, Love wrote:

> I roped, threw, tied, bridled, saddled, and mounted my mustang in exactly 9 minutes from the crack of the gun. The time of the next nearest competitor was 12 minutes and 30 seconds. . . . Right there the assembled crowd named me Deadwood Dick and proclaimed me champion of the western cattle country.

The growing number of settlers in the West finally put an end to the long trail drives. Both farmers and ranchers began to fence in their land with barbed wire. By the end of the 1880s there was no longer enough open grassland or water to support large herds of moving cattle. Also, railroads had been built all over the country by then, and cattle could be transported more easily by cattle car than by being driven along the trails.

The final blow to the classic cowboy way of life was the extremely severe winter of 1886–87, which caused thousands of cattle to starve or freeze to death. Many ranchers lost most of their stock. The ranchers who survived this "great die-up" realized that they needed to have smaller herds and keep them on their own land. In 1890 L. Bradford Prince, the governor of New Mexico, wrote:

> After years of experience, the owners of cattle have demonstrated that the business of cattle-ranging on the open ranges is not profitable. There is a disposition to smaller holdings and to confine the cattle in inclosed pastures. Prominent ranchmen express the opinion that 500 cows confined in pastures will produce more profit than 5,000 on the open ranges.

When the trail drives ended, many cowboys had to look for other kinds of work. Some took jobs completely different from what they had done before, such as farming or working on the railroads. Nat Love, for example, became a Pullman porter in 1890. He enjoyed the chance to work with people, he said, and, according to Philip Durham and Everett Jones, believed that the job "offered a challenge to an ambitious man."

Other black cowboys continued to work on ranches or even went into the ranching business themselves. One experienced black cowboy who became a ranch owner was Daniel Webster Wallace, nicknamed "80 John" because for many years he worked for a ranch that used "80" as its cattle brand. Wallace saved part of the money from each of his pay-

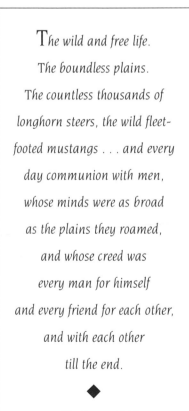

The wild and free life. The boundless plains. The countless thousands of longhorn steers, the wild fleet-footed mustangs . . . and every day communion with men, whose minds were as broad as the plains they roamed, and whose creed was every man for himself and every friend for each other, and with each other till the end.

◆

—Nat Love, 1907

Bill Pickett, shown here on his horse Spradley, could force a steer to the ground using his teeth. His boss, Zack Miller, called him "the greatest sweat-and-dirt cowhand that ever lived." (Courtesy Western History Collections, University of Oklahoma Library, Phillips Collection)

checks and used it to buy cattle. When new land in Texas became available for homesteading in 1885, Wallace purchased two sections. He continued to work for other ranchers for another 14 years and then left to work full time for himself. Eventually he owned 1,200 acres of land and 600 cattle. He won the respect of both blacks and whites in his county and even became a financial advisor to some of them.

A number of ex-cowboys earned money by showing off their skills in rodeos or Wild West shows. Beginning in the 1890s, rodeos grew from amateur contests held for cowboys' amusement to professional shows put on to entertain paying audiences. African-American cowboys who tried to join rodeos often found that prejudice barred them from competition or at least from winning major prize money. They would be given horses that others considered too wild to ride or, at the other extreme, horses that would not buck at all. (If a horse would not buck, its rider could not win any points to count toward a prize.) Some rodeos kept blacks out by requiring a hefty entrance fee that few could afford. If a black cowboy did win a rodeo contest, judges often found some way to disqualify him. Some blacks got around these problems by pretending to be Mexican. A black cowboy named Mose Reeder, for example, called himself "Gaucho the Corral Dog."

Nonetheless, some black cowboys did find fame as rodeo or show performers. The best known of these was Bill Pickett. Pickett first joined the 101 Ranch in Oklahoma in 1900, when it was large and employed many cowboys. One of the ranch's owners, Zack Miller, called Pickett "the greatest sweat-and-dirt cowhand that ever lived—bar none."

When the 101 Ranch started a traveling western show around 1905, Pickett joined. He worked with cowboys such as Will Rogers, who later became famous as a humorist, and Tom Mix, who became a star in early Western movies.

Bill Pickett became known for a method of throwing a steer called bulldogging (now termed steer wrestling). He did not invent this technique, but he applied it in such an original way that many people thought he had. Traditional bulldoggers wrestled a steer to the ground with their bare hands, but that was not challenging enough for Bill Pickett. Instead, Pickett brought down the steer with his teeth. Fred Gipson, who wrote a book about the 101 Ranch called *Fabulous Empire*, described Pickett's act this way:

> He piled out of his saddle onto the head of a running steer, sometimes jumping five or six feet to tie on. He'd grab a horn in each hand and twist them till the steer's nose came up. Then he'd reach in and grab the steer's upper lip with his strong white teeth, throw up his hands to show he wasn't holding any more, and fall to one side of the steer, dragging along beside him till the animal went down.

Pickett's technique would strike people as cruel today, and steer wrestlers in modern rodeos are not allowed to use it. Still, it thrilled many an audience in the early part of this century. In 1971, 39 years after his death, Pickett became the first African American to be elected to Oklahoma City's Cowboy Hall of Fame. His achievements stand as a reminder of the skill of all the other, mostly nameless, black cowboys whose "sweat and dirt" helped to tame the West.

NOTES

p. 87 "Don't leave out . . ." William Loren Katz, "The Black West (Seattle, Wash.: Open Hand Publishing, 1987), p. xi.

p. 88 "firmly believed . . ." Paul W. Stewart, Wallace Yvonne Ponce, *Black Cowboys* (Broomfield, Colo.: Phillips Publishing/Black American West Museum, 1986), p. vii.

p. 92 "The point of their history . . ." Philip Durham, Everett L. Jones, *The Negro Cowboys* (New York: Dodd, Mead, 1965), p. 12.

p. 92   "During the halcyon . . ." Kenneth Wiggins Porter, *The Negro on the American Frontier* (New York: Arno Press and the New York Times, 1971), p. 521.

p. 92   "If it weren't . . ." Quoted in Durham and Jones, p. 24.

p. 93   "surpassed any man . . ." Quoted in Philip L. Durham, Everett L. Jones, *The Adventures of the Negro Cowboys* (New York: Bantam, 1969), p. 41.

p. 93   "Imagine . . . riding your horse . . ." Nat Love, *The Life and Adventures of Nat Love* (Los Angeles, 1907), quoted in Stewart and Ponce, p. 37.

p. 95   "I acted like . . ." Quoted in Durham and Jones, *Adventures*, p. 68.

p. 96   "Sometimes when they brought . . ." Quoted in Stewart and Ponce, p. 84.

p. 96   "an unusually adventurous . . ." Love, quoted in Katz, *Black West*, p. 150.

p. 98   "a typical frontier city . . ." Love, quoted in Katz, *Black West*, p. 150.

p. 98   "I roped, threw, tied . . ." Love, quoted in Stewart and Ponce, p. 37.

p. 99   "The wild and free life . . ." Love, quoted in Durham and Jones, *Adventures*, pp. 93–94.

p. 99   "After years of experience . . ." Quoted in Durham and Jones, *Adventures*, p. 109.

p. 99   "offered a challenge . . ." Durham and Jones, *Negro Cowboys*, p. 204.

p. 100, 101   "the greatest sweat-and-dirt cowhand . . ." Fred Gipson, *Fabulous Empire*, quoted in Katz, *Black West*, p. 160.

p. 102   "He piled out of his saddle . . ." Quoted in Durham and Jones, *Adventures*, p. 97.

8

"Struggling People Working Hard": Homesteaders, 1879–1914

Cowboys saw some of them walking up the Chisholm Trail, carrying everything they owned on their backs or packed on those of patient donkeys. Others waited on river banks with their bags and bundles for a steamboat to come and carry them. In 1879 20,000 to 40,000 African Americans migrated from the South to new homes in the West. Most were heading to

Kansas, where they hoped to build homes and farms and start a new life.

They called themselves the Exodusters. Like the Hebrew people in the Bible who fled slavery in Egypt in a migration called the Exodus, they were turning their backs on a way of life that had become intolerable. Many did not know about the "dust" part of the supposed paradise they were headed to—the soil swept up constantly by the scouring winds of the Great Plains—but even when they discovered this problem, very few turned back. Hard as it proved to be, they felt that life on Plains homesteads was better than life in the South.

African Americans had been hopeful about the changes that occurred just after the Civil War. For the first time they had the opportunity not only to vote but to hold political office. Their rights were at least partly protected by federal troops stationed throughout the South. But this period, called Reconstruction, made white southerners feel very resentful. The southerners said the soldiers treated them like a conquered people. They complained that some of the black people elected to office were not qualified. They objected to having their lives controlled by northerners whose chief motives seemed to be revenge and profit.

Even while the federal troops remained, white southerners found ways to take out their resentment on African Americans. In 1867 they organized a secret group called the Invisible Empire of the South, better known as the Ku Klux Klan (KKK). Its members, masked and covered with white sheets to look like ghosts, rode out at night to terrorize or even murder blacks who committed "crimes" such as voting.

Henry Adams, an African-American Civil War veteran who lived in Shreveport, Louisiana, organized a committee of 500 African Americans in 1869 to document the mistreatment of blacks in the South. The committee sent about 150 representatives throughout the southern states to investigate the conditions under which African Americans lived. They wanted to find out, Adams said later, "whether there was any

State in the South where we could get a living and enjoy our rights." The investigators found that conditions were just as bad as they had suspected—and often worse. "The people was still being whipped, some of them, by the old owners, the men that had owned them as slaves, and some of them was being cheated out of their crops."

After receiving the investigators' reports, Adams's committee tried to decide what to do. In 1874 they organized a "colonization council," which sent letters to President Ulysses S. Grant and to Congress documenting mistreatment of African Americans. They asked either for help in securing their rights or for land and money to be given them so that they could settle as a group in unoccupied western lands. Failing that, they asked for money to pay for emigrating to Africa. None of their requests was answered.

> The whole South—every state in the South—had got into the hands of the very men that held us slaves. . . . The largest majority of the . . . white people that [had] held us as slaves treats our people so bad . . . that it is impossible for them to stand it. . . . We said there was no hope for us and we better go.
>
> ◆
>
> —Henry Adams, in testimony to a Senate committee, 1880

Reconstruction ended in 1877 when the last army troops left the South. Southerners were once again free to run their own lives—and those of the African Americans living in the South. White leaders quickly passed laws that deprived blacks of most of the rights that they supposedly had won at the end of the Civil War. Many of these "Jim Crow laws" remained in effect until the 1950s or 1960s.

With the end of Reconstruction, Henry Adams later told a Senate committee, "We lost all hopes. . . . We looked around and we seed that there was no way on earth, it seemed, that we could better our condition" in the South. Leaving the area seemed to be the only answer. Although some members of Adams's group still wanted to go to Africa, a majority decided that a better opportunity lay in the West. Black conventions in New Orleans and Nashville reached the same conclusion.

The African Americans chose Kansas as a possible new home because they had heard that both cheap land and jobs were available there. According to the Homestead Act of 1862, anyone could claim 160 acres of public land for a small fee if the person would live on the land for five years and "improve" it by starting a farm or a ranch. Large amounts of such land existed in Kansas. In addition, railroads were extending across the state, and workers were needed to lay tracks and do other jobs. There were also jobs in the cattle industry, handling the huge herds that the cowboys were driving to Abilene and other Kansas cow towns. Because of the state's need for workers, Kansas government and railroad officials promised to help African Americans who moved there.

By the thousands, African Americans from all over the South began heading for Kansas in 1879. Adams's group sponsored some of the migrants. Others were led by Benjamin ("Pap") Singleton, who had been born a slave in Nashville, Tennessee, in 1809. Around 1873 Singleton bought land in Baxter Springs, Kansas, then went back to Tennessee to seek African Americans willing to move there. For the next several years, he made many trips to the South, advertising his colony with posters and promoting it in speeches. In all he brought in some 7,500 settlers. Singleton later bragged to a Senate committee, "*I* am the whole cause of the Kansas migration!" He gave himself more credit than he deserved, but he certainly was a leader in the Exoduster movement.

Not all African-American leaders approved of the black exodus. Frederick Douglass, the best-known African American spokesperson of the time, opposed the movement, saying that black people should give democracy a little more time to work in the South. Blanche Kelso Bruce, a prominent

As a leader of the Exoduster movement, Benjamin ("Pap") Singleton brought thousands of African Americans to Kansas in 1879 to set up homesteads and begin a new life free of the oppression they suffered in the South.   (Courtesy Kansas State Historical Society)

African-American man who had been a senator from Mississippi during Reconstruction, feared that the move would weaken the concentration of blacks, and thus their potential political power, in the South. But other leaders, such as Professor Richard T. Greener, dean of the law school at all-black Howard University in Washington, D.C., supported the movement.

Southern white opinion was less divided. Most southerners were horrified to see their cheap labor force departing. Some tried to stop the Exodusters by force. They threatened to sink any steamboat that carried emigrants north. They forbade transportation companies to sell tickets to African Americans. Black travelers on the roads were arrested as vagrants—or worse. One group caught an emigrant, cut both his hands off, and threw him in his wife's lap, saying, "Now go to Kansas and work!"

Less violent southerners appealed to Congress. They claimed that the Republican Party had sponsored the migration in order to bring masses of black voters into Kansas. A Senate committee held a hearing in 1880 to investigate their accusations. Both Henry Adams and Benjamin Singleton testified at the hearing. Their words made it clear that conditions in the South and the hope for a better life were the only reasons why African Americans were leaving.

These men's moving testimony did not keep the majority of the committee, who were Democrats and supported the South, from continuing to believe that the Republicans had created the Exoduster movement. Only the African Americans who had left their homes knew better. Their feelings were expressed in a poem called "Exode" by W. H. Stillwell, which appeared in the Chicago African-American newspaper *Inter-Ocean*.

> Whence came these dusky legions,
> Braving the wintry wind?
> For our snow-bound, icy regions

These fleeing, dusky legions
Leave a summer land behind.

They fly from the land that bore them,
As the Hebrews fled from Nile;
From the heavy burthens o'er them;
From the unpaid tasks before them;
From a serfdom [slavelike condition] base and vile.

Unfortunately, most of the Exodusters brought little with them except their determination. A reporter named Henry King described one group of black refugees in an article in the June 1880 issue of *Scribner's Monthly*:

One morning in April, 1879, a Missouri steamboat arrived at Wyandotte, Kansas, and discharged a load of colored men, women and children, with divers [various] barrels, boxes, and bundles of household effects. . . . They were of all ages and sizes . . . their garments were incredibly patched and tattered, stretched, and uncer-

Surrounded by their few household goods, these Exodusters wait for a steamboat to carry them to Kansas. (Courtesy Library of Congress)

tain . . . and there was not probably a dollar in money in the pockets of the entire party. . . . They stood upon the wharf shivering. . . . They looked like persons coming out of a dream.

Kansas was almost as unprepared for the migrants as the migrants were for Kansas. Some Kansans drove the Exodusters out of their towns, but most scrambled to help. Henry King noted that "temporary shelter was speedily provided for" the Exodusters, and "food and facilities for cooking it were furnished them in ample measure." Kansans, both white and black, organized a Freedmen's Relief Association and an Emigration Aid Society to provide support for the new arrivals. The aid society collected money all over the country, taking in more than $100,000 in all.

Most of the Exodusters did not rely on charity any longer than they had to. King wrote:

> The closing autumn [of 1879] found at least 15,000 of these colored immigrants in Kansas. Such of them as had arrived early in the spring had been enabled to do something toward getting a start, and the thriftier and more capable ones had made homestead-entries [filed papers to claim land for homesteads] and contrived, with timely aid, to build cabins. . . . .
>
> Numerous cabins of stone and sod [soil with grass roots] were constructed. . . . In many cases, the women went to the towns and took in washing, or worked as house-servants . . . while the men were doing the building. Those who could find employment on the farms about [near] their "claims," worked willingly and for small wages, and in this way supported their families . . . ; others obtained places on the railroads, in the coal-mines, and on the public works at Topeka. Such as got work at any price, did not ask assistance; those who were compelled to apply for aid did it slowly, as a rule, and rarely came a second time.

This spirit of determination and hard work helped African Americans survive hardship all over Kansas and other Plains states. Faced with dust storms, droughts, and insect plagues, some black homesteaders (like the whites dealing with the same problems) gave up and moved into the cities, where they hoped life would be easier. The one option most would not consider, however, was returning to the South. Some emigrants told John H. Johnson, an African-American lawyer from St. Louis, that they "would rather go into the open prairie and starve there than go to the South and stand the impositions that were put upon them there."

Other African-American homesteaders hung on and eventually became prosperous farmers. Perhaps the most spectacularly successful was Junius G. Groves of Edwardsville, Kansas, who became nationally known as the Potato King. Groves came to Kansas in 1879 with only 90 cents in his pocket. At first he and his wife worked for another farmer as sharecroppers, renting land in return for a share of the crop they raised on it. The Groveses raised enough crops to have produce left over. They sold their surplus, saved the money they earned, and after several years were able to buy their own farm.

Thanks to his careful preparation of the soil, Groves grew up to 396 bushels of potatoes per acre of land. Farmers around him sometimes produced only 25 bushels per acre. He grew other vegetables as well, including onions, corn, and cabbage. He used the money he made from these bumper crops to add more acreage to his farm. By 1910, the Groves farm contained 2,100 acres and included a 22-room house. It was said to be one of the finest farms in Kansas.

As Kansas began to fill up, some of the Exodusters and other African-American migrants who came after them moved on to Nebraska, which also needed workers. Some set up homesteads, while others took jobs on the railroad or in the smelting and meat packing industries.

Lacking wood, midwestern homesteaders built homes of stone or sod (hard-packed earth held together with grass roots). This photograph, taken by S. D. Butcher, shows the Shores family of Custer County, Nebraska, who became prosperous farmers and well-known musicians.   (Courtesy Nebraska Historical Society, Solomon D. Butcher Collection)

Other African-American settlers found similar mixtures of hardship and success in other Western states. In 1881, for instance, the Chicago _Evening Journal_ reported:

> The thousands of Negroes who went to Indiana a year ago from North Carolina and Virginia have been absorbed, and are distributed all over the state. The resident Negroes supplied them with clothing, furnished them . . . with food, and found homes for them in the farming districts. Their labor was needed, and they are doing well.

The last hope of taking over a large area and making it more or less exclusively African American came with the land rush to settle Oklahoma, the area that had been Indian Territory. Many African Americans were already living there when the area was opened for general settlement in 1889.

Nicodemus, An All-Black Town

Many of the Exodusters believed that their best hope lay in establishing a society as separate as possible from that of European Americans. In 1879, for instance, an editorial in an African-American newspaper in Indiana called *The Colored Visitor* stated:

> What is to be the final destiny of the colored race of this country is a problem. . . . I boldly assert that the only practical plan for ever settling the question is for the black men of this country to select one of the territories of this government and to gain by legal means possession of it, and then go into it, and settle it up and go to work and build towns, churches, and everything else necessary, and thus form a state of their own. In this way, and in this way only, can the Negroes make of themselves a happy and prosperous people.

Following this plan, some of the emigrants to Kansas set up all-black towns and settlements. Perhaps the best known was Nicodemus, named after a slave mentioned in the Bible. W. R. Hill and a group of African Americans from Topeka established it in Graham County, northwest Kansas, in 1877. Advertisements for Nicodemus promised:

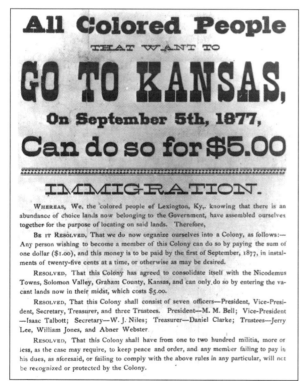

Advertisements like this lured Exodusters to Nicodemus and other all-black Kansas towns. (Courtesy Kansas State Historical Society)

> Cheap Homes! Cheap Lands! . . . The best lands in all Kansas . . . in the beautiful Solomon Valley . . . the garden of the Northwest. Thousands of acres of Wild Lands, Improved Farms and Stock Ranches for sale.

Conditions in the town's first year were hardly what the advertisements led settlers to expect. Willianna Hickman, a Kentuckian who came to Nicodemus with her family in March 1878, described her first horrified sight of the town:

> We were two days on the way [from Ellis, where the railroad left them, to Nicodemus], with no roads to direct us save deer trails and buffalo wallows. We traveled by compass. At night the men built bonfires and sat around them, firing guns to keep the wild animals from coming near. . . .
>   When we got in sight of Nicodemus the men shouted, "There is Nicodemus." . . . I looked with all the eyes I had. I said, "Where is Nicodemus? I don't see it." My husband pointed out various smokes coming out of the ground and said, "That is Nicodemus." The families lived in dugouts. The scenery to me was not at all inviting and I began to cry.

As the months passed, Hickman became "reconciled to [her] home," a homestead 14 miles west of Nicodemus. In the town and the surrounding homesteads, settlers replaced their dugouts with more permanent homes of stone or sod, bricklike blocks of earth held together by the tough roots of the prairie grasses. Hundreds of new residents arrived as the full tide of the Exodus poured into Kansas. By 1880, Nicodemus had about 650 people and a business district of some 35 buildings, including a post office, general store, school, and church. Five years later it even had its own newspaper and baseball team.

Nicodemus lost some of its businesses when the Kansas Pacific Railroad failed to build a proposed spur track that would have connected the town with the railroad. The town continued to do reasonably well, however, until the late 1930s. But the depression and the war years, during which many rural people of all races abandoned their farms for life in the cities, weakened it. Today only a few hardy families keep Nicodemus and its proud history alive.◆

They were the former slaves and allies of the Five Civilized Tribes, especially the Seminole, Creek, and Cherokee. These Native American groups had accepted the blacks more or less as equals and some had intermarried. Many of the African Americans who lived in Indian Territory shared the feelings of O. S. Fox, who wrote in 1879:

> The opportunities for our people in that country far surpassed any of the kind possessed by our people in the U.S. . . . It is nonsense for any Afro–American to emigrate to Africa or anywhere else if he can make a living in the Indian Territory.

Ten thousand more African Americans were among the wave of approximately 50,000 immigrants who poured across the border when the territory was opened for general settlement on April 22, 1889. Oklahoma's black population almost tripled between 1890 and 1910.

African Americans established 27 all-black towns in Oklahoma, much like Nicodemus and the other black towns that the Exodusters had set up in Kansas. The best known of the Oklahoma towns was Boley. Officials of the Fort Smith and Western Railway created the town to serve as a station and water stop for trains going to Guthrie, the territory's capital. They named it after W. H. Boley, the railroad's roadmaster.

Even though Boley had been planned by European Americans, the town and its government consisted of African Americans. The town poet, a man known only as Uncle Jesse, wrote this song in honor of Boley:

> Say, have you heard the story,
>   Of a little colored town,
> Way over in the Nation
>   On such a lovely sloping ground?
> With as pretty little houses
>   As you ever chanced to meet,
> With not a thing but colored folks

> A-standing in the streets?
> Oh, 'tis a pretty country
>   And the Negroes own it, too
> With not a single white man here
>   To tell us what to do—in Boley.

Boley was established on the land of an African-American woman, Abigail Barnett McCormick, in 1904. Within a year it had a population of 200, applied for incorporation to become a town, and held its first election. It soon had a business district, a cotton gin, a sawmill, a newspaper, and a high school. In 1905, African-American educator Booker T. Washington visited Boley and called it "the most enterprising, and in many ways the most interesting of the Negro towns in the United States."

Two years later, Boley's population numbered 2,000. After that, however, a combination of a political climate that was increasingly repressive to blacks and a fall in the price of cotton, on which Boley's economy depended in part, greatly slowed the rate of immigration to the town. Eventually many of its people left for larger cities. Like Nicodemus, Boley survives today, but its population is low.

An African American named E. P. McCabe had hopes of making Oklahoma an all-black state, perhaps with himself as governor. McCabe had been the state auditor of Kansas from 1883 to 1887 and was the first African American to hold this post. Both blacks and whites called him "the recognized leader of his race in the West." He led thousands of African Americans to Oklahoma during the 1889 land rush in the hope of building black voting power there. He helped to create another all-black town, Langston.

McCabe eventually became deputy auditor of Oklahoma, but that was as far as he and his dream of African-American power could go. European Americans, needless to say, had no intention of letting Oklahoma become an all-black state. Indeed, its laws became as repressive as those of the South.

Blacks in effect were forbidden to vote, and segregation was enforced—right down to telephone booths, something no other state had required. The newspaper in Boley complained, "Not only don't they want the Negro to not vote but want him to get off the earth as well." McCabe eventually moved to Chicago, where he died in poverty in 1920.

As black hopes for Oklahoma faded, some African Americans moved even farther west and set up all-black towns in other states. For example, Reverend Allen Allensworth, a former chaplain with the "Buffalo Soldier" 24th Infantry, founded a black town in the fertile San Joaquin Valley of southern California. After retiring from the army in 1906, Allensworth traveled around the country for two years, lecturing on the theme of African-American self-sufficiency, before settling in Tulare County, California. There he established Allensworth, the only all-black town in the state, in 1908.

At its height, Allensworth contained about 300 people and boasted a school, library, and train station. It flourished until 1914, when two disasters struck: Reverend Allensworth died, and the town's water table dropped below a level that wells could reach. Deprived of the water they needed to raise their crops, most of the small farming community's residents moved away. Today the site of the town, including a school and several other restored buildings, is a state historic park.

In all, more than 60 all-black towns were founded in the United States, mostly between about 1870 and 1910. Most of these towns lasted until the 1930s, when a combination of drought and economic depression turned them more or less into ghost

People [in Dearfield] got along well. It was a peaceful sort of situation: struggling people working hard; they didn't have time for trouble. There was a spirit of helpfulness.

◆

—Eunice Norris, early resident of Dearfield, Colorado, an all-black town founded in 1910 towns. Only a few survive, monuments to an enterprising African-American dream.

NOTES

pp. 105–106 "whether there was . . ." Testimony to Senate investigating committee in 1880, quoted in William Loren Katz, *Black People Who Made the Old West* (Trenton, N.J.: African World Press, 1992), p. 151.

p. 106 "The people was still being whipped . . ." Testimony, quoted in Milton Meltzer, ed., *The Black Americans: A History in Their Own Words 1619–1983* (New York: HarperCollins, 1984), p. 131.

p. 106 "We lost all hopes . . ." Testimony, quoted in Meltzer, p. 133.

p. 106 "The whole South . . ." Testimony, quoted in Meltzer, pp. 133–134, and William Loren Katz, *Eyewitness: A Living Documentary of the African American Contribution to American History* (New York: Simon and Schuster, 1995), p. 298.

p. 107 "*I* am the whole cause . . ." Testimony, quoted in William Loren Katz, *The Black West* (Seattle, Wash.: Open Hand Publishing, 1987), p. 175.

p. 109 "Now go to Kansas . . ." Elizabeth L. Comstock, quoted in Arna Bontemps and Jack Conroy, *Anyplace but Here* (New York: Hill and Wang, 1966), p. 65.

pp. 109–110 "Whence came these dusky legions . . ." *Chicago Inter-Ocean*, March 12, 1881, quoted in Bontemps and Conroy, p. 53.

pp. 110–111 "One morning in April . . ." Henry King, "A Year of the Exodus in Kansas," *Scribner's Monthly*, June 1880, quoted in Katz, *Eyewitness*, p. 310.

p. 111 "temporary shelter was speedily provided . . ." King, quoted in Katz, *Eyewitness*, p. 311.

p. 111 "The closing autumn . . ." King, quoted in Katz, *Eyewitness*, p. 311.

p. 112 "would rather go . . ." Quoted in Katz, *Black West*, p. 175.

p. 113 "The thousands of Negroes . . ." Chicago *Evening Journal*, February 7, 1881, quoted in Bontemps and Conroy, p. 68.

p. 114 "What is to be the final destiny . . ." *The Colored Visitor*, August 1, 1879, quoted in Dierdre Mullane, ed., *Crossing the Danger Water: Three Hundred Years of African-American Writing* (New York: Doubleday, 1993), p. 327.

p. 115 "Cheap homes! Cheap lands! . . ." *The Western Cyclone*, Nicodemus, Kansas, July 15, 1886, quoted in Mullane, p. 326.

p. 115 "We were two days on the way . . ." Quoted in Dorothy Sterling, ed, *We Are Your Sisters: Black Women in the Nineteenth Century* (New York: Norton, 1984), p. 375.

p. 115 "reconciled to [her] home" Quoted in Sterling, p. 376.

p. 116 "The opportunities for our people . . ." *Afro-American Advocate*, quoted in Katz, *Black Indians: A Hidden Heritage* (New York: Atheneum, 1986), p. 147.

pp. 116–117 "Say, have you heard the story . . ." Quoted in Katz, *Black West*, p. 251.

p. 117 "the most enterprising . . ." Quoted in Katz, *Black West*, p. 248.

p. 117 "the recognized leader . . ." Quoted in Katz, *Black West*, p. 256.

p. 118 "Not only don't they want . . ." Quoted in Katz, *Black People*, p. 168.

p. 118 "People [in Dearfield] . . ." Quoted in Katz, *Black West*, p. 298.

9

"You Are Wanted, Come": City Dwellers, 1885–1914

Young man, if you are about to finish at Howard, Fisk, Wilberforce, or Hampton [top African-American universities], do not hang around Washington waiting for a chance to feed on government pap [take government support money], or go to Boston to wait [work as a waiter] in a hotel, and thus sink what little manhood you had at first, but come this way [West]—come to bear trial, come to work and wait, come to wait and win, come determined to be or die trying. You are wanted, come.

It took a long time for those words to be written. Only in the last quarter of the 19th century did significant numbers of African Americans begin to feel that the call of "Go west, young man!" that had lured so many European Americans away from the East in earlier years also applied to them. And even then, many went west only because life in the East—at least in the South—had become intolerable.

But go they did. Their number was never very large; even in 1890, only 4 percent of African Americans lived west of the Mississippi. Still, by 1910, they amounted to almost a million people. The bulk of them lived in Texas and Oklahoma, but African Americans were scattered throughout the western states by the beginning of this century.

By 1890—only four years after the New York *Freeman* wrote "You are wanted, come"—historians consider that the western frontier was closed. European Americans had achieved their "manifest destiny" of spreading their way of life across North America. Farms and small ranches, tidily enclosed by barbed-wire fences, covered the once open plains where buffalo and dusty herds of Texas cattle had roamed. Railroads transported people and goods from one side of the continent to the other in days instead of weeks or months. Bustling towns and cities had replaced hastily built settlements of miners, cowboys, or railroad workers.

To be sure, frontier-style life still went on in some places, and African Americans still took part in it. At the turn of the century in Cascade, Montana, for example, strapping 6-foot, 200-pound Mary Fields still delivered the mail in a stagecoach or, if the weather was bad enough, on foot through the snow. Black cowboys were hard at work on western ranches. Open land still existed that would later contain all-black towns such as Boley and Allensworth.

Increasingly, though, African Americans, like European Americans, were moving to the cities. Life was usually easier there than on homesteads, and the range of job opportunities was greater. Blacks faced more segregation in cities than they had on the open frontier, however. Segregation in western cities was less rigid and formal than in the East, especially in the South, but its enforcement, as well as their own preference in many cases, led African Americans in western cities to form communities that paralleled but usually did not mix with those of European Americans.

African-American communities in most large western cities had their own newspapers, which built a sense of pride and unity by describing the achievements of local blacks and carrying social and church news. The newspapers also chronicled abuses of civil rights and the communities' attempts to correct these abuses. Black western newspapers in the late 19th century included the Chicago *Inter-Ocean*, the San Francisco *Elevator*, the Topeka *American Citizen*, and the Denver *Statesman*.

As did most settlers in the West, the African Americans also had an active social life. Much of it centered around black churches, such as the African Methodist Episcopal and First Baptist churches in San Francisco. Other mainstays of black western social life were the less formal religious gatherings called camp meetings, fraternal organizations such as the Freemasons, and social clubs, which sponsored both humanitarian and self-improvement activities. The Chicago *Evening Journal* noted in 1881 that recently arrived African Americans in Indiana were "social in their habits, and fond alike of dancing, religious meetings, and political discussion."

As with African-American communities in the East, women formed the center of black communities in western cities. Dr. Ruth Flowers, one of the first black women to earn a medical degree, wrote in the early

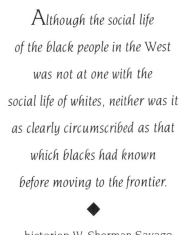

Although the social life of the black people in the West was not at one with the social life of whites, neither was it as clearly circumscribed as that which blacks had known before moving to the frontier.

◆

—historian W. Sherman Savage, 1976

1900s that "black women were the backbone of the church, the backbone of the family, they were the backbone of the social life, everything." They organized churches, orphanages, schools, and literary societies. Many ran small businesses. They were more likely than white western women to be well educated and active in local politics. Most black western women preferred city to country life, and in some cities, such as Los Angeles and Denver, they made up a majority of the African-American population in the late 19th century.

At that time African Americans, both men and women, shared with European Americans a great interest in business and economic advancement, and blacks had a better chance to achieve such advancement in the West than in the East. A number of blacks in western cities owned their own businesses, ranging from barbershops, restaurants, and laundries to Barney Ford's huge Inter-Ocean hotels in Denver, Colorado, and Cheyenne, Wyoming. Ford's hotels promised "the squarest meal between two oceans" and hosted black and white guests from presidents on down.

African Americans who had succeeded in business in the West made a point of encouraging other blacks to join them. In 1905, for example, citizens of Colorado Springs formed a chapter of the National Negro Business League. Their statement of formation said in part:

We believe that the time has come for the colored people to enter more largely into business pursuits by means of individual as well as co-operative efforts as the surest and most speedy way to gain earn-

Many [African-American] women [in Seattle in the late 19th century] nursed their dreams that someday things would be better, if not for them, then for their children. . . . They wanted to believe that this was still the land of opportunity.

◆

—Esther Hall Mumford, 1980

Barney Ford's Inter-Ocean Hotel in Denver promised "the squarest meal between two oceans" and had many prominent guests. (Courtesy Denver Public Library, Western History Department)

ings from invested capital, and to afford employment for our race. . . . Resolved, That we take steps to present the wonderful undeveloped agricultural and mineral resources of Colorado to desirable colored citizens who may be induced to settle in this state, bring[ing] with them capital, brains, and pluck.

Professional fields, on the other hand, were usually denied to blacks. Historian W. Sherman Savage reports that even as late as 1900, fewer than 100 African Americans in western states were known to work in the professions of teaching, medicine, and dentistry. The one profession that did have a reasonable number of blacks was the ministry, which had 600 black members in the West.

As leaders in the progressive African-American community in San Francisco had done even before the Civil War, leaders of western black communities in the late 19th century struggled to gain the civil rights that their people still so often lacked. Mary Ellen Pleasant in California and E. P. McCabe in Oklahoma both filed suit against transportation companies for refusing to carry them, for example. (Pleasant won a judgment of $700, though a higher court reversed this; McCabe lost.) In 1874 John Jones waged a successful campaign to desegregate Chicago schools. In other cases, communities worked together to fight abuses such as school segregation.

Blacks were still, at least informally, discouraged from voting in some parts of the West, and they were too few in number for their votes to have much effect in most places. African-American communities in Colorado, Kansas, Oklahoma, and Iowa, however, contained enough voters by the late 19th century to have an effect on local and sometimes state politics. This was particularly true in Kansas, where the Exoduster movement had created a relatively large African-American population. Iowa produced a notable black politician, Alexander Clark, who, according to historian W. Sherman Savage, "was one of the important figures in the Republican party for more than a quarter of a century." Known as "the Orator of the West," Clark was said to be second only to Frederick Douglass in speaking skill.

African Americans may have been missing from the fictional West of novels, movies, and television shows, but in the real West of history they played a definite role. They helped to map unexplored territories, build roads and railroads, raise crops, and herd cattle. They cleared the land and kept the peace. They ran barbershops, laundries, restaurants, hotels, and a host of other businesses. In short, they did as much as anyone to create a new civilization in this untamed land. They did it against greater odds than most, facing all the hardships of frontier life plus the additional hardship of being rejected, even sometimes attacked, because of the color of their skin.

In return they achieved, not full equality or even fair treatment, but at least a better chance for advancement than most would have had if they had stayed in the East. Historian W. Sherman Savage has concluded:

> For most black people, the West was not the Promised Land. But neither were its restrictions as severe as those which they had known in the South and the East. On balance, the West has given blacks an opportunity to make a better life for themselves.

Americans of all races need to revise their understanding of the myth of western settlement to make room for these black pioneers. Recognizing their role can, as Colin Powell said of the Buffalo Soldier monument, "motivate us to keep struggling until all Americans have a seat at our national table, until all Americans enjoy every opportunity to excel, every chance to achieve their dream."

NOTES

p. 121 "Young man . . ." New York *Freeman*, May 15, 1886, quoted in Dierdre Mullane, ed., *Crossing the Danger Water: Three Hundred Years of African-American Writing* (New York: Doubleday, 1993), p. 325.

p. 123 "Although the social life . . ." W. Sherman Savage, *Blacks in the West* (Westport, Conn.: Greenwood Press, 1976), p. 191.

p. 123 "social in their habits . . ." Chicago *Evening Journal*, February 7, 1881, quoted in Arna Bontemps and Jack Conroy, *Anyplace but Here* (New York: Hill and Wang, 1966), p. 68.

p. 124 "black women were . . ." Quoted in William Loren Katz, *The Black West* (Seattle, Wash.: Open Hand Publishing, 1987), p. 281.

p. 124 "Many [African-American] women nursed their dreams . . ." Esther Hall Mumford, *Seattle's Black Victorians* (Seattle, Wash., 1980), quoted in Katz, *Black West*, p. 315.

p. 124 "the squarest meal . . ." Quoted in William Loren Katz, *Black People Who Made the Old West* (Trenton, N.J.: Africa World Press, 1992), p. 104.

pp. 124–125 "We believe the time has come . . ." *Booker T. Washington Papers*, quoted in Katz, *Black West*, p. 188.

p. 126 "was one of the most important . . ." Savage, p. 166.

p. 126 "the Orator of the West," Leola N. Bergmann, "The Negro in Iowa," *Iowa Journal of History and Politics* 46 (January 1948), quoted in Savage, p. 165.

p. 127 "For most black people . . ." Savage, p. 199.

p. 127 "motivate us to keep struggling . . ." Speech given on July 25, 1992, quoted in Catherine Reef, *Buffalo Soldiers* (New York: Holt, 1993), p. 74.

Appendix: The Growth of the Western Black Population

STATE	1840	1850	1860	1870	1880	1890	1900
Arizona				26	155	1,357	1,848
California		902	4,086	4,272	6,018	11,322	11,045
Colorado			48	436	2,435	6,215	8,570
Idaho				60	53	201	940
Iowa		333	1,069	5,762	9,516	10,485	12,693
Kansas			627	17,108	43,107	40,710	52,003
Minnesota	188	29	259	759	2,564	3,683	4,950
Montana				183	346	1,400	1,523
Nebraska			82	789	2,385	8,913	6,289
Nevada			45	367	488	242	134
New Mexico		22	85	172	1,015	1,936	1,160
North Dakota				94	113	373	455
Oklahoma						21,000	55,000
Oregon		207	128	346	487	1,186	1,106
South Dakota				94	288	541	465
Utah		50	59	118	232	588	672
Washington			30	207	325	1,602	2,514
Wisconsin	196	636	1,171	2,133	2,702	2,444	2,542
Wyoming				183	346	1,400	1,523
TOTAL	384	2,179	7,689	33,109	72,575	115,598	165,432

Total Population in Thousands *

*Does not include data for Texas or territories not yet states.   Source: Bureau of the Census

Chronology

1492	First expedition of Christopher Columbus; crew includes black navigator, Pedro Alonzo Niño
1493	Columbus brings first African slaves to New World
1526	Slaves from Ayllón colony in Florida escape, forming first permanent nonnative settlement in land that would eventually belong to the United States
1539	Estevanico guides expedition to Southwest to find Seven Cities of Cibola; is killed by Zuñis
1607	Palmares and Jamestown founded
1619	First African slaves brought to Jamestown
1660s	Southern colonies establish slavery for life (rather than for a period of indenture)

1779	Jean-Baptiste Pointe du Sable establishes trading post on site of Chicago
1787	Northwest Ordinance forbids slavery in Northwest Territories
1803	Louisiana Purchase doubles size of United States
1804	Lewis and Clark expedition begins
1817–58	Seminole Wars
1820	Missouri Compromise passed
1829	Mexico abolishes slavery in its territories
1835	Texas begins fighting for independence from Mexico
1845	Texas becomes a slave state
1846	Division of Oregon Territory with Britain; Mexican War begins
1848	Treaty ending Mexican War gives California and Southwest to United States; gold discovered in California
1850	Compromise of 1850 passed; California becomes a free state; Jim Beckwourth discovers pass across Sierra Nevada
1854	Kansas-Nebraska Act passed; elections and fighting in Kansas; Republican Party formed
1855	First California Colored Convention held
1857	Dred Scott refused freedom by Supreme Court

1860	Abraham Lincoln elected president; South Carolina secedes from Union
1861	Civil War begins
1865	Civil War ends
1866	Four all-black "Buffalo Soldier" regiments created
1867	Trail drives of beef cattle from Texas to Kansas along Chisholm Trail begin
1869	Henry Adams organizes committee to investigate treatment of African Americans in the South
1870	Seminole-Negro Indian Scouts organized in Texas
1877	End of Reconstruction; Nicodemus founded
1879	Exoduster movement to Kansas; Buffalo Soldiers begin pursuit of Victorio
1886–87	Severe winter causes "great die-up" of cattle, marks end of long trail drives
1889	Indian Territory opened for general settlement
1890	Frontier considered closed

Further Reading

Banks, Leo W. "The Buffalo Soldiers." *Arizona Highways*, January 1995, pp. 35–37. Focuses on the Buffalo Soldiers' activities in Arizona.

Billington, Monroe Lee. *New Mexico's Buffalo Soldiers 1866–1900*. Niwot: University Press of Colorado, 1991. Describes Buffalo Soldiers' service in New Mexico, including battles against Victorio and daily life in the forts. Difficult reading.

Bonner, Thomas D. *The Life and Adventures of James P. Beckwourth*. Lincoln: University of Nebraska Press, 1972. Autobiography of the most famous black mountain man. Difficult but exciting reading.

Bontemps, Arna, and Jack Conroy. *Anyplace but Here*. New York: Hill and Wang, 1966. Describes migration of African Americans to various cities. Has chapters on Jean-Baptiste Pointe du Sable, Jim Beckwourth, John Jones, and the Exoduster movement. Some parts are fictionalized.

"Colonel Allensworth's Black Colony in the San Joaquin Valley." *Sunset*, September 1983, pp. 48–49. Describes the black town of Allensworth in California and its present existence as Colonel Allensworth State Historic Park.

Cromwell, Arthur, Jr. *The Black Frontier*. University of Nebraska Television, 1970. Good overview of African-American activities on the frontier.

Drotning, Philip T. *Black Heroes in Our Nation's History*. New York: Washington Square Press, 1970. History of African Americans, with an emphasis on their role as soldiers; includes chapters on explorers, early settlers, soldiers in the Indian wars, and cowboys.

Durham, Philip, and Everett L. Jones. *The Adventures of the Negro Cowboys*. New York: Bantam Books, 1969. Shorter, less scholarly version of authors' *Negro Cowboys*. Lively reading. For young adults.

Durham, Philip, and Everett L. Jones. *The Negro Cowboys*. New York: Dodd, Mead, 1965. Detailed, exciting account of African-American cowboys.

Jackson, George F. *Black Women Makers of History: A Portrait*. Oakland, Ca.: GRT Book Printing, 1985. Includes a chapter on 19th-century African-American women in California and Nebraska and a few other sketches of African-American women pioneers. Biographical emphasis. For young adults.

Jones, Archie H. "The First Chicagoan." *Country Beautiful*, November 1966, pp. 31–35. Detailed account of Jean-Baptiste Pointe du Sable, the African American who was the first to build a permanent settlement on the site of Chicago.

Katz, William Loren. *Black Indians: A Hidden Heritage*. New York: Atheneum, 1986. Describes the often close relationship between African Americans and Native Americans and profiles pioneers of mixed African and native descent. For young adults.

———. *Black People Who Made the Old West*. Trenton, N.J.: Africa World Press, 1992. Series of biographical sketches presents the most interesting people described in Katz's *Black West*. For young adults.

———. *The Black West*. Seattle: Open Hand Publishing, 1987. Detailed description of African Americans' activities in the 19th-century West, enlivened by many primary source quotations. Best book on the subject for general readers.

———. *Eyewitness: A Living Documentary of the African American Contribution to American History*. Revised edition. New York: Simon & Schuster, 1995. African-American history text, featuring many lengthy primary source quotations, has three chapters wholly or partly devoted to African Americans in the West.

Lapp, Rudolph M. *Blacks in Gold Rush California*. New Haven: Yale University Press, 1977. Interesting but somewhat difficult book includes European Americans' reaction to African Americans in gold rush California, blacks' daily life in the mines and the cities (especially San Francisco), the three California conventions, and more.

Leckie, William H. *The Buffalo Soldiers*. Norman: University of Oklahoma Press, 1967. Detailed history of the four "Buffalo Soldier" regiments, focusing on the 9th and 10th Cavalries and their pursuit of raiding Native Americans. Somewhat difficult but exciting reading, with many primary source quotations.

Morganthau, Tom. "Slavery: How It Built the New World." *Newsweek*, special issue, Fall–Winter 1991, pp. 66–69. Overview of the role of

African-American slaves in developing the Americas, beginning with the first Spanish settlements.

McGinty, Brian. "A Heap o' Trouble." *American History Illustrated*, May 1981, pp. 35–39. Biographical article about Dred Scott, the slave whose attempt to gain freedom through the courts on the grounds that he had been taken voluntarily to a free state resulted in a disastrous rejection of African-American rights by the U.S. Supreme Court in 1857.

O'Connor, Richard. "'Black Jack' of the 10th." *American Heritage*, February 1967, pp. 14–15, 102–107. John J. Pershing, America's highest-ranking military officer in the years just after World War I, was nicknamed "Black Jack" because he had served with, and highly praised, the "Buffalo Soldier" 10th Cavalry regiment. Article describes Pershing's exciting years with the 10th.

Porter, Kenneth Wiggins. *The Negro on the American Frontier*. New York: Arno Press and the New York *Times*, 1971. Lengthy collection of Porter's scholarly articles, focusing on the Seminole Wars and the activities of blacks in Texas. Difficult reading.

Reef, Catherine. *Buffalo Soldiers*. New York: Holt, 1993. Overview and exciting accounts of the activities of the all-black 9th and 10th Cavalries, from their formation through the Spanish-American War. For young adults.

Savage, W. Sherman. *Blacks in the West*. Westport, Conn.: Greenwood Press, 1976. Scholarly book includes interesting information on the work, social life, and civil rights struggles of African Americans in the 19th-century West. Difficult reading.

Smithsonian Institution. *Blacks in the Westward Movement*. Washington, D.C.: Smithsonian Institution Press, 1975. Well-illustrated, booklet-size overview of African Americans in the West.

Stewart, Paul W., and Wallace Yvonne Ponce. *Black Cowboys*. Broomfield, Colo.: Phillips Publishing/Black American West Museum, 1986. Short biographical sketches of African-American cowboys in the late 19th and early 20th centuries. Illustrated with many old photographs.

Thybony, Scott. "Against All Odds, Black Seminole Won Their Freedom." *Smithsonian*, August 1991, pp. 90–100. Interesting account of the Seminole Wars, the Seminole-Negro Indian Scouts who served with the Buffalo Soldiers, and their descendants today.

Tuesday Magazine editors. *Black Heroes in World History*. New York: Bantam, 1969. Includes chapters on African-American explorers Esteban (Estevanico) and Jean-Baptiste Pointe du Sable. For young adults. Parts are fictionalized.

Index

Italic numbers indicate illustrations.